BOOKS
MAKE A
HOME

BOOKS
MAKE A
HOME

ELEGANT IDEAS FOR STORING
AND DISPLAYING BOOKS

DAMIAN THOMPSON

RYLAND
PETERS
& SMALL

LONDON NEW YORK

To Kit and Roger, who marked me with books,

and to Peter, who always has a bookmark to hand.

Designer Paul Tilby
Editor Rebecca Woods
Picture research Emily Westlake
Head of production Patricia Harrington
Art director Leslie Harrington
Publishing director Alison Starling

Indexer Diana LeCore

Published in 2011 by
Ryland Peters & Small Ltd

20–21 Jockey's Fields
London WC1R 4BW

519 Broadway, 5th Floor
New York, NY 10012

www.rylandpeters.com

10 9 8 7 6 5 4 3 2 1

ISBN: 978 1 84975 187 2

A catalogue record for this book is available
from the British Library.

Library of Congress Cataloging-in-Publication
Data

Thompson, Damian, 1962-
  Books make a home : elegant ideas for storing
and displaying books / Damian Thompson.
       p. cm.
  Includes index.
  ISBN 978-1-84975-187-2
  1. Books in interior decoration. I. Title. II.
Title: Elegant ideas for storing and displaying
books.
  NK2115.5.B66T49 2011
  747'.9--dc23

            2011022760

Printed in China

Designed to occupy a minimal amount of wall space, this modular
'Paperback' wall system for storing books and other objects horizontally
comes from the Dutch-based Studio Parade. Each dynamic unit, which
includes a wall panel and 13 sliders, holds around 80 books.

CONTENTS

OPPOSITE In this London interior, the architrave round the alcove bookcase reflects the restrained classicism of the chimneypiece and the cornice.

RIGHT The library of German naturalist Alexander von Humboldt (1769-1859) contains many traditional features, such as busts of eminent figures, a globe, a table used for storing maps and engravings and, in the distance, a telescope.

BELOW When your library doubles as a ballroom – as it does at Stradbally Hall in County Laois, Ireland – glass doors help protect the first editions from whirling crinoline.

INTRODUCTION

'When I have a little money I buy books. And if any is left, I buy food and clothing.' With the endless stream and variety of entertainments competing for our attention today, few of us could sign up to the dictum of Erasmus, the Renaissance humanist. Nonetheless, books still enrich our lives in myriad ways. From the comfort of an armchair, we can travel the world, acquire a skill and plunge into the past. The anthologist Alberto Manguel has described reading as the compass that guides us in our self-discovery and in our exploration of the world. We look at other people's shelves to provide clues to their interests and characters; for similar reasons, we are loath to throw away our own books because they feel part of our identity: Benjamin Franklin even described himself as a book that God would copyedit after his death. There's another good reason why we should hold on to books, at least according to Canadian novelist Robertson Davies: 'A truly great book should be read in youth, again in maturity and once more in old age, as a fine building should be seen by morning light, at noon and by moonlight.' All this getting and never-letting-go provides us with challenges of storage and display, whether we live in a modern urban loft, a Victorian semi or a Georgian villa.

Good design is often about achieving economy of form, whether it's a perfectly balanced Anglepoise lamp, a cast-iron Victorian radiator, panelled folding shutters or a structured leather sofa. Unaligned horizontal shelves in the built-in bookcase add unexpected dynamism to the pared-back scheme.

OPPOSITE ABOVE In this Milan library, the bookshelves are unusual in being narrowest at top and bottom (where CDs are stored) and widest in the middle. In any event, it is the basking Buddha that is bearing the brunt of the sun, not the precious books.

OPPOSITE BELOW When the mouldings are as refined as this, colour would be a distraction. This integrated bookcase echoes the form of a column, a point underlined by the marble bust and dentil cornice above it.

VANDALS VS VENERATORS

In this concise guide, words and pictures work in tandem to provide design solutions for every kind of space, taste and size of collection. Touring the rooms of a typical house, you'll discover a host of techniques for stacking, shelving and closeting books. But how you choose to store, display and organize them is not merely a matter of interior design, of course; it's also down to personal disposition. For some, books are simply chunks of paper, cloth, cardboard, glue and thread, banal containers for the holy writ of words. I refer to those sinners who dog-ear the corners of pages and lick their fingers in turning over a new leaf. Visiting the house of my cousin, a serious book collector, my bad habit is to leave my paperback face down and splayed open; whenever I return, it has always been closed with a bookmark discreetly slid in place. It is

shaming, but I am in good company. The chemist Sir Humphry Davy would tear out pages as he finished reading them, while Dr Johnson's biographer, James Boswell, came across the great lexicographer in clouds of dust pounding his old books with hedger's gloves. At the other end of the spectrum are the purists, whose libraries are climate-controlled and dehumidified; they carefully catalogue their idols, line them up on the shelf and handle them with kid gloves. In *Ex Libris*, the journalist Anne Fadiman cites the case of one New York collector who won't allow his wife to open the blinds till after dark 'lest the bindings fade'. An investment analyst by day, he 'buys at least two copies of his favourite books, so that only one needs to be subjected to the stress of having its pages turned'.

THE END OF THE BOOK?

Whether you'd place yourself at either extreme or somewhere in the middle, is there any point investing in shelves and bookcases in the digital age? When a Kindle can easily hold some 1,500 titles, perhaps all our books are headed for landfill. It is true that publishers are facing the biggest upheaval to their industry since Gutenberg invented his press in 1439, but reports of the death of the book have been greatly exaggerated. Some 80,000 books were published in Britain alone last year. It is true that writers can self-publish online, cutting out the middle man and thereby boosting what they earn. But publishers are a key quality filter; they have expertise about what constitutes good writing and how to reach readers; their editorial, design and picture-research staff bring experience and add quality to the finished article. Hand-held devices are a boon to the traveller, no question, but traditional books have visual and tactile qualities that are irreplaceable. Indeed, the net effect of digital publishing may well be that 'real' books will become more expensive, more like the 'niche' products they were in the past; but the process may force us to value them more, to become more discriminating about their aesthetic qualities. As the philosopher Alain de Botton has argued: 'We should stand to swap a few of our swiftly disintegrating paperbacks for volumes that proclaim, through the weight and heft of their materials, the grace of their typography and the beauty of their illustrations, our desire for their contents to assume a permanent place in our hearts.'

LEFT Celebrated Danish designer Nanna Ditzel, who died in 2005, maximized the drama of the 2 metre-high sash windows in her Copenhagen home by stripping back the walls containing them and surrounding the deep jambs with flush bookshelves. One needs to be careful storing books so close to an outside wall as fluctuations in temperature can lead to condensation and, eventually, mould.

The circular mirror, and its echo of the 'rising sun' motif, adds a Japanese flavour to the bedroom of Sigolène Prébois, co-founder of quirky web shop Tsé & Tsé Associates. The room is dominated by a no-nonsense floor-to-ceiling bookcase whose long shelves slot into uprights via housing joints. This and the rough-and-ready ladder are softened by delicate patterned fabrics.

BOOKS AS DECORATION

'I WOULD BE MOST CONTENT IF MY CHILDREN GREW UP TO BE THE KIND OF PEOPLE WHO THINK DECORATING CONSISTS MOSTLY OF BUILDING ENOUGH BOOKCASES' *(Anna Quindlen)*. Books not only enrich the mind – they are increasingly designed to appeal to the eye. From towers to tableaux, from colour-coded stacks to leather-bound tomes on tables, the book's ability as an aesthetic aid should not be underestimated.

An ottoman-cum-footstool in the living room of stylist Ulrika Lundgren in Rika, the Netherlands, offers space for informal piles of books – and for one's feet as one lies back and reads them. This is a room where décor is minimal; with the white walls as a backdrop, shapes, masses and volumes (including the book stacks) sculpt the famous Dutch light as in a Vermeer painting.

In the Philadelphia home of Anthropologie creative team Kristin Norris and Trevor Lunn, there is a pleasing graduation in height from the stack of coffee-table books on the folding footstool to the tall screen-fronted cabinet. The high arms of the antique high-backed settee offer seclusion from distractions, but its uncompromising shape would make it uncomfortable for prolonged reading.

'Books are not made for furniture, but there is nothing else that so beautifully furnishes a house.' When the Congregationalist preacher Henry Ward Beecher wrote these words in the mid-19th century, most educated homes of the middling sort possessed a small library of sombrely bound volumes neatly corralled into a parlour, study or alcove. Their decorative potential, in other words, was limited. Nowadays, despite competition from other media, new titles continue to pour out of publishing houses, which often put as much effort into making their form desirable as they do into ensuring their content is worthwhile. An eye-catching jacket helps a book stand out in a crowded marketplace. And while such elements as decorative endpapers, heavy paper stock and glossy photographs all add to a publisher's costs – and therefore the price consumers pay for the end

ABOVE These book stacks do not block views of the fire, because it's in a raised grate. The shallow shelves propping up pictures could also be used for face-out cover display.

LEFT A statuesque pile of books consisting of four towers at 90-degree angles ensures that spines can be seen from any vantage point. Why not secure a sheet of glass on top to improvise a side table?

RIGHT The boards of hard-backs are often beautifully tooled or gold embossed. Note how effectively the sheaves of corn on the bottom spine harmonize with the seat cover.

ABOVE LEFT The set of the complete plays of Anton Chekhov contains enough wisdom for a lifetime, but the stack is not so imposing as to dwarf the simple vase with its sprig of berries alongside.

ABOVE RIGHT A publisher's series is always collectable, even if the titles are not first editions. This set from the 1950s showcasing adventure novels, explorer's memoirs and traveller's tales is very appealing, with signs of the zodiac marching down the spines in contrasting colours.

RIGHT 'Judge not a book by its cover' is the admonishment on this brass Art Nouveau book holder, ideal for holding reference books on a desktop.

OPPOSITE When forming stacks, think carefully about scale and proportion, as architect François Muracciole has done in his Paris apartment, in matching size of volume to African stool.

product – books are, relative to income, cheap compared to the past. This can mean that bibliophiles have large numbers of these aesthetically pleasing objects and not enough shelf space to house them.

PILES AND PLATFORMS

If that's the case, make a virtue out of necessity. An artfully positioned stack of books can lead the eye towards an unassuming but finely executed pencil sketch in the corner of the room; equally it can divert attention away from a window with its eyesore of a tower block beyond. Speaking of which, a single 'skyscraper' of 30 or more books in the corner creates a powerful vertical accent among beds, low coffee tables and sprawling sofas, but they should be arranged in strictly diminishing order of size for added stability. Ideally, too, books should

be regularly rotated into and out of this arrangement, so that bindings are not crushed over time. There are practical downsides, it must be said, not least the difficulty in retrieving the copy you want. Hi-fi equipment and Ming vases should be kept well away

What better spot for dedicated followers of fashion to work their way through a stack of old *Vogue*s and *Elle*s than a classic Eames plastic chair of 1950?

OPPOSITE ABOVE LEFT
Eschewing shelves and keeping one's clutter low down near the edges of a room is a good strategy if one is renting and soon moving on. Moreover, blank upper walls foster contemplation.

OPPOSITE ABOVE RIGHT
A simple Perspex table makes a neat house for piles of reading matter. The additional support from below even means the furniture is capable of bearing more weight.

OPPOSITE BELOW RIGHT
If you have a small room, deep bookshelves can make one feel positively claustrophobic. One option is to have a very narrow shelf for pictures at dado level and stack your books centrally.

IF YOUR HOUSEHOLD INCLUDES PETS OR TODDLERS, FORGET STACKS

from the topple radius, and if your household includes pets or toddlers, you might as well forget the idea.

Large books that rarely need to be consulted can form an eye-catching base for a glass table-top – likewise serving as pedestals for speakers or telephones. For these kind of semi-permanent arrangements, think about positioning the books to create chromatic rhythms with, say, red- or black-coloured spines recurring at regular intervals. Nabokov wrote: 'In reading one should notice and fondle details.' The same applies to little tableaux that can be created on coffee tables, side chairs and cabinets. An antique lamp looks great propped up on a couple

the support. For the kind of vignettes that we're currently discussing, though, you should forget the large-format coffee-table titles and the heavy cast-iron brackets or massive mahogany Ls that they would call for. Given the relatively simple physical forces at work, product designers have carte blanche to let their imaginations rip. Witty examples include a bold 'A' and 'Z'; 'pushing' and 'leaning' Soviet Realist-style workers; and a Chinese dragon's head at one end, with its tail emerging at the other end of the row. Most eye-catching of all is two 'halves' of a goldfish bowl, complete with live tropical specimens, which leave what they enclose frankly upstaged.

ABOVE LEFT No doubt Barbara Cartland would have approved of these faded red leather novels tied up with string and strewn with roses.

ABOVE RIGHT Drape diaphonous scarves and bright beads over a stack of books on a chair – an instant snapshot of the owner's personality.

RIGHT Yellows, pinks and oranges are hard to get right, but everything is anchored by the stripy abstract painting and the two bottom-most spines.

OPPOSITE, ABOVE AND BELOW In organizing one's books by colour, it's easier on the eye to follow the spectrum, having cool colours (blues and greens) separate from warm ones (reds and yellows) – ideally the mid-temperature hues (purples and pinks) form a visual bridge. The approach is especially effective on a rough matt background such as this exposed-brick wall.

of matching faded leather tomes, while two low equal piles of books at either end of a bench in a hallway might echo the symmetry of the pictures or wall sconces on the wall above. In the warm months, when the fire is never lit, fill a wicker basket with a stack of art books and place it on a waxed wooden floor by the hearth – you instantly perk up a moribund spot.

BOOKENDS

Bookends mean that you can enliven narrow surfaces, such as console tables, mantelpieces or reasonably wide window-sills, with little vertical runs. These simple devices work by a mixture of gravity and friction – the taller and heavier the block, and the rougher the contact between bookend and underlying surface, the stronger

OTHER IDEAS

What other techniques are there for showcasing the purely aesthetic qualities of your books? In some shelving units, it is possible to have the occasional shelf oriented on a slant, with a lip, just like a long lectern, so that you can face some covers outwards; this can also be done on regular shelves – just as bookshops do to promote titles with strong sales potential – breaking up an endless sea of spines with graphically bold or pictorially memorable jackets. Just like in an art gallery, one can 'rotate' regularly those you display. Organizing by colour offers a hit of pure pop-art pleasure; not only does the rainbow effect offer a wonderful focal point, but one can find new correspondences between subjects (on my own

shelves, now that an Odilon Redon monograph, Phaidon's three-volume *Design Classics* and a book on loft living are rubbing yellow shoulders, it sparks off new directions in lateral thinking). This approach works best with chunky hardbacks.

Finally, in some minimalist schemes, I have seen books arranged so that their tails and fore-edges face outward. All right, you can argue that, particularly if they're all squashed in higgledy-piggledy, the textural effect of pages going in all directions can create an interesting abstract sculpture, a contrast from the ordered, cool neutrality elsewhere. But – sorry to state the blindingly obvious – I do want to be able to find a book without pulling apart my collection every time.

OPPOSITE, FAR LEFT On a painted wrought-iron, marble-topped sewing table, a pencil sketch of a poppy echoes the outline of a tin lamp. The open book functions as a landscape picture, the black-edged boards serving as a thin frame.

THIS PAGE AND OPPOSITE RIGHT While nothing could steal the limelight from events designer Jo Berryman's fabulous sunburst mirror, her alcove-width ladder bookcase comes close. Topped by a bulbous designer hi-fi speaker, the five face-out shelves offer the chance for a continually evolving display.

An elegant four-seater chesterfield cunningly masks the wall-to-wall low cabinet behind by matching its height exactly. Books therefore seem to float between the sofa and the powerful abstract and framed light fittings on the wall above. Two horizontal stacks support a reclining statuette and an antique bottle, respectively.

LIVING ROOMS

'I FIND TELEVISION VERY EDUCATING. EVERY TIME SOMEONE TURNS THE SET ON, I GO INTO THE OTHER ROOM AND READ A BOOK.' (*Groucho Marx*) Alternatively, you could banish the TV from your living room – its presence there is not obligatory. Whether you opt for alcoves filled with shelves, a wall of books or a designer statement, this is the place where we have the most options. But beware! It's also 'front of house' – where your reading tastes will be on display to all and sundry.

The horizontal lines of Dieter Rams' slim and sleek 'Vitsoe' system – the most desirable of all the minimal free-standing shelves – seem to usher in the 18th-century Dutch tiled woodstove in the corner. Note the torchlike light hanging from a ceiling flex for close examination of spines.

RIGHT Although they don't exactly align, both the bookcase and the double set of sash windows are divided into eight horizontal sections – the ladder also has the same number of gaps between the rungs. This kind of attention to ratios does matter. The downlighters on the stanchions have multiple hinges.

Since we are now turning to what is, for most people, the biggest room in their home, the one they spend the most time in and the place where they usher in their visitors, planning is crucial. Will the television or hi-fi system take pride of place, or will you banish other media to different parts of the house, making a stand for the primacy of reading? If you decide that you want to combine books with ornaments, do your shelves have sufficient depth to place objects in front? Or perhaps you could opt for a shelving unit that combines shelving with open-fronted cabinetry.

It's important to calculate exactly how much space your books are going to take up, by how much they are likely to swell over the coming years, and how you are going to organize them. Unless you possess only novels, a strictly alphabetical-by-author approach won't work, since you will have big design

LOOK AT YOUR MANTELPIECE SHELF TO HELP YOU DECIDE ON THE THICKNESS OF THE BOARDS

books next to diminutive paperbacks. The critic Susan Sontag once told the *New York Times* that 'it would set my teeth on edge to have Pynchon next to Plato'.

ALCOVES AND BUILT-IN SHELVES

People who live in a house that's 19th-century or older may well have a fireplace and a chimneybreast in their living room. The alcoves formed on either side are effectively an open-fronted box and, therefore, an open invitation to build in some shelves for books. Using movable brackets that

OPPOSITE LEFT It looks dramatic to flow bookshelves right round a doorway, but take care not to swamp the architectural features. Here, two mighty uprights help to keep the entrance defined, and what might have been an oppressive grid is disrupted by an irregular alcove and a decorative chandelier that fractures the light.

OPPOSITE RIGHT The acids present in wood pulp mean that pages degrade. Given different qualities of paper, and editions of various vintages, a bookcase with tail edges facing out can present an abstract sculpture of limitless off-white tinges.

LEFT The square pillar in the corner presented a challenge to the designer of this alcove – one solved by placing vases, a tiny oil painting and a dynamic bronze in the shallow sections. Blue-spined books complement the terracotta of the unglazed busts beneath the cornice.

BELOW The innovative, apparently floating 'Nook' coffee table, by David Pickett, features an integrated bookshelf.

slot into vertical rails, one can create adjustable shelving here, but the finished effect can be unsightly. It's better, in my view, to opt for simple shelves supported left and right with wooden blocks screwed into the wall and painted the same colour to blend in. Planks cut to size, and then either

oiled, stained or painted, have a natural affinity with what they hold. (The word book is thought to derive from the old German word for 'beech' and, besides the lexical link, pages are made from pulped timber.) Look at your mantelpiece shelf to help you decide on the thickness of the boards; bear in mind, too, the weight of books, and the fact that fairly thin shelves will need vertical struts to avoid unsightly sagging. To make the shelves appear to float, one can screw the brackets into the wall and cover them with plaster; plastering over the shelves, too, softens them, creating a series of Arab-style recesses that appear to grow organically from the wall.

Unless the room's proportions are grand, it is good practice to leave around two-thirds of the wall space, either above or below, free so that all the sideways volume offered by the alcoves is not lost. One can enhance the inherent symmetry of matching niches by placing similar-sized pictures above your books.

OPPOSITE With its rivets and weathered ceiling boards, this living room feels like it's below decks – the ship's model, stripy cushions and nautical flag pictures only add to the salty flavour. Bookshelves cover one whole wall, but the small scale of the items they hold makes the vaulted space more approachable.

ABOVE Do you shudder when you see books leaning against each other? Bad for them it may be, but in conjunction with this corrugated ceiling in the Sussex home of architectural salvager Eliza Barnes, it somehow looks good.

LEFT In a whole wall of built-in shelves, alternate thin with thick uprights, as here, to create a visual rhythm and stop them looking bland.

ABOVE The ceiling height of this loft in Covent Garden, London, allows for a second set of shelves on a gallery accessed via a spiral staircase hidden behind the office area at far left. A long bench in the mezzanine has chrome supports that appear to extend the uprights from below. There, an Eames leather armchair offers the ideal reading spot.

LARGE AND OPEN-PLAN SPACES

Many people like the idea of a large loft-style living area, or perhaps a double-height living room in which the attic has been sacrificed to create a more vaulted space. The danger is that one can feel dwarfed in such surroundings; fortunately, books can be enlisted to help. An entire wall of them can make the scale seem more human; after all, books are designed to be held in the hand, and the variegated mass of colour that an expanse of spines creates helps make a large wall look less oppressive and more approachable. 'Walls lined with books have a richness of texture and colour, as well as being wonderful insulation,' says interior

THE DANGER IS THAT ONE CAN FEEL DWARFED IN LOFTY SURROUNDINGS

designer John Stefanidis; they also reduce echo in a cavernous space. Because this approach is fairly flamboyant, consider the effect on the rest of the décor. In an otherwise baroque space, one with ornate wallpaper, expressive paintings and fancy mouldings, a regular grid of functional shelving serves as an effective counterpoint. But if the room is quite minimal in flavour, one might need to inject some visual interest in one's wall of books – perhaps by alternating thin and thick

ABOVE The governing principle of these shelves is rectangles of varying heights but the same width – an idea that combines brilliantly with the collection of miniature antique keyboards sitting above. Objects sit in front of books, and some shelves are occupied by glassware, offering variations in depth. The narrow double doors are a necessary compromise.

on both sides and not too densely packed means that light can penetrate and one can catch glimpses through to the space beyond. When one wants to have the option of screening off, say, a kitchen from the living area, a more dramatic intervention is to combine bookshelves with sliding doors. That requires engineering know-how, however, and ideally the input of an architect.

BOOKCASES

The great disadvantage of built-in shelving and cabinetry is that you can't take it with you when you move, unlike the next two types of literary store we'll

stanchions for a vertical rhythm, interspersing the books with eye-catching objects, or painting the wall behind an accent colour. If, at reasonably regular intervals, you lay the odd stack of titles horizontally, this also adds syncopation. Whatever idea you adopt, you will need to solve how to access the books in the upper tier, whether via a ladder on castors, a mezzanine gallery or even – as in one eccentric solution I've seen – a bosun's chair attached to a chain-and-pulley system fixed to the ceiling to hoist the reader up to higher shelves.

Another way to break up a large space is to use a shelving unit as a partition. Since, by necessity, this will only be attached to the wall at one end, pretty much all the weight has to be supported by the floor. Check that it can take it. Having such a shelf open

OPPOSITE LEFT The tripod might not be the ideal form for creating neat stacks of books, but this repurposed pan stand certainly looks elegant, despite the modest materials from which it is made. The turned-out feet echo the armchair's.

OPPOSITE RIGHT In her Paris home, stylist Marina Coriasco has used a light-admitting partition bookcase – seen behind a marble-topped Saarinen table – to screen off a reading area populated by two plump Louis XVI-style fauteuils and an 'Arco' lamp.

In this detailed look at Marina Coriasco's interior, we can see how the airiness of the converted electrics factory (see previous picture) has been maintained. Light pours through the hollow rectangles of her simple partition shelves, which have been left as untreated MDF, with only the simplest of architraves. Ostrich feathers, glass lanterns and semi-opaque plastic boxes all offer different takes on translucency. The bamboo ladder serves as an impromptu seat-back for the leather pouf.

consider. Any conventional bookcase worth its salt will employ a peg-and-hole system to make shelves adjustable, and if it is tall, the facility to attach it to the wall to avoid tipping. But there are other options, too. Ladder bookcases have four feet and taper upwards, with 'treads' that are deepest at the bottom and shallowest at the top. Because of their open construction, they are effective if you wish to combine books in horizontal piles with, say, house

OPPOSITE From the tall brick chimneybreast to the buttoned sofa in a textured olive synthetic, this New York interior is a celebration of mid-20th-century style. The 1950s cabinet makes an ideal spot to house first editions of a similar vintage.

BELOW Now that the hard drives of most new televisions can store feature films, the DVD shelf can be filled with books instead.

RIGHT Nickel shelves can look too utilitarian, but here three factors help: the sisal floor offers textural contrast, the red wall adds warmth and the metallic uprights are topped with unexpectedly decorative finials.

BELOW RIGHT Since books and magazines are very heavy, one must be careful not to overload glass shelves: around three piles, the weight spread horizontally, is about right.

LEFT Behind a 'streamlined' armchair stands display furniture salvaged from a draper's shop. The glass doors fold up into the shelf cavity in these 'barrister's bookcases', as they are traditionally called – law students would once have used them to keep their expensive volumes of case law protected from dust.

OPPOSITE The 'Bibliochaise', from Italian designers Nobody & Co, is an Art Deco-flavoured armchair library for those who like to literally immerse themselves in a good book – or make that five linear metres of books.

plants, vases, lamps and other objects. Leaning bookcases tend to be fairly minimal and light in their design, with a relatively small footprint, because they employ the wall behind as their structural support. At their most basic, the point of contact is solely at the top; in more sophisticated examples, the shelves extend at progressive distances behind the side supports, touching the back wall all the way down. Barrister bookcases, originally designed to house large-format volumes of case law, have for each tier of shelving a glass door that swivels up into the case itself; such a case should be designated for the rare books in your collection.

Inside corners always create problems when it comes to housing books: when two cases meet at right angles, do you overlap them, leaving an inaccessible unused space, or do you leave one short and necessitate reaching into a hard-to-see cavity? One elegant solution is to install the kind of revolving carousel that they use in bookshops.

OPPOSITE ABOVE LEFT
Being stared at by this soapstone object brings to mind the Emerson quote: 'What's a book? Everything or nothing. The eye that sees it all.'

OPPOSITE BELOW
This uniform grid of shelves looks great against the contrasting pattern of the brick courses. The Russel Wright tableware in the central cavities introduces pleasing shapes and reminds us of the depth of the room space.

OPPOSITE ABOVE CENTRE
Owning small children or pets rules out certain kinds of book display: toddlers chasing next to a tottering tower is an accident waiting to happen. Likewise worn, expensively tooled leather bindings, laid horizontally, will be an open invitation to a cat, especially if near a radiator, or as here, on a sun-drenched windowsill. If the books aren't precious, however, the ensemble can look very endearing.

OPPOSITE ABOVE RIGHT
If you mix open shelving with door-fronted cabinets, one can hide away clutter and ugly bumf next to objects meant for display, such as these organic stoneware vases and books. The asymmetric position of the cabinets and their different widths gives dynamism and visual rhythm to a wall, and because you open the doors by pushing the fronts, there are no distracting knobs.

ABOVE A custom-made wall unit – which offers storage for a hi-fi and an integrated air-conditioning unit behind the pierced panels – serves as the backdrop to a battered leather 'Contour' sofa by De Sede. Though perhaps not optimally arranged here, the layout of the rectangular recesses means that books look good stored horizontally or vertically. The neutral shades of the ceramics offset the eye-catching spines.

REDUCING BOOKS' VISUAL IMPACT

Not everyone wants to have their books to the fore – either for reasons of style or personality. A lifetime's worth of reading says a lot about your tastes, interests and past history, and some people feel uncomfortable about that degree of exposure. At one extreme, books can be hidden behind wooden doors, but glass, with its reflections, normally repels casual browsers. Metal barriers of various kinds, from a lattice of chicken-wire to metal stays, also have the effect of bringing to prominence the furniture housing the books. In a muted scheme, which derives subtle effects from harmonious variations of one or two shades, a wall of books can be too brash a focal point. After all, publishers design the spines of their titles

ABOVE Modular shelving systems like Vitsoe's are easily adaptable to awkward spaces. Shrewd use of mirrors makes the top-heavy arrangement seem less monolithic.

OPPOSITE Industrial chic meets modern classics. A plush 'Charles' sofa by B&B Italia and a sinuous coffee table by Piero Lissoni contrast with box-like shelves on heavy central brackets that are spot-on in the warehouse setting.

specifically to stand out from their neighbours – the bookshop browser is being prodded into turning buyer. That commercial imperative adds up to a lot of visual noise for would-be minimalists. If you really want people to notice your discreet antique creamware jug against its backdrop of Elephant's Breath estate emulsion, you might want to consider wrapping your books in, say, a variety of off-white papers.

FREE-STANDING SHELVES AND DESIGNER OPTIONS

Though some are made of wood, free-standing shelving systems are often these days made of metal, and many of them are direct descendants of the classic tubular-steel furniture of Modernist luminaries such as Charlotte Perriand and Marcel Breuer in the 1920s. In a contemporary interior, metal has the advantage of being both strong and lightweight, meaning that in smallish rooms, especially, one does not feel hemmed-in by massive, hulking forms, and the architectural space is more legibly articulated. The disadvantage is that metal shelving can look both clinical and utilitarian. Who wants to put their feet up in a DIY centre? The effect can be counteracted by offsetting metal units with gestural abstract paintings, a decorative mirror or warm textures, such as a squashy leather sofa with velvet cushions. Many of these systems – from Ikea's inexpensive 'Ivar' shelves to Dieter Rams's classic 'Vitsoe 606' at the top end of the market – are also modular, meaning that they are made out of small repeatable elements that can be put together in a variety of different ways. That flexibility is a real plus and, assuming the manufacturers don't go out of business, you can invest in additional 'modules' as and when you need them.

The structural principles underlying the basic bookshelf are so simple that, inevitably, designers continue to come up with more and more outlandish concepts. One can find a veritable forest of branching

ABOVE The lintel around this alcove, or blocked-up doorway, adds polish to this corner, as does the way the second shelf aligns with the dado rail. The spines cohere beautifully with the sophisticated neutral colour scheme, and the limed candlesticks, the sinuous wrought-iron table and the Baroque finials all add up to French country style – except it's an English house.

OPPOSITE To break up the space, architect Michael Neumann incorporated this unit – with open storage front and back, and push-front cupboards to the sides – in an open-plan Manhattan apartment. Books provide a welcome blast of colour in the monochrome space, and the width of the 'floating' shelves has been carefully matched to that of the floorboards.

RIGHT Just like fractals, furniture of great complexity can be built out of relatively simple components. The Los Angeles-based J1 Studio has come up with the 'T Shelf' (or triangle shelf) system, which is available as a set of eight triangles in Baltic birch plywood. When the sets are combined, they can be endlessly reconfigured either as a table or other floor-standing unit, or else hung on the wall as a sculptural storage unit. The triangles, which can be painted, are joined together using a simple system of zip ties.

LEFT The great advantage of Contraforma's 'Quad', by Finnish designer Nauris Kalinauskas, is that its square format contains niches of varying sizes, meaning that you can house your desert-island CDs, DVDs, magazines, coffee-table books and paperbacks within one stained-oak-veneer unit.

RIGHT In an improvised solution in keeping with this laid-back summerhouse, miniature platforms are wedged into a long plank prepared for lap joints. The resulting tower of books creates a pattern of jazzy white dashes against the outsize boards, and the dotty rug stops everything becoming too stripy.

ECCENTRIC SHELVING

Eccentricity is in the eye of the beholder, of course, but there are any number of whimsical, eye-catching and downright impractical options available for book owners wishing to make a visual statement. Odd forms, such as a plastic cow, a harp and a seesaw, have all been revamped to hold books, and perhaps the punchiest example of this genre is Ron Arad's steel outline of the United States, with each of the states forming a recess (Texas holds the most). People cannibalize objects, too, whether it's a grid of shelves formed by wheel-free skateboards or just a hollowed-out television filled with books (spot the polemical point). On the same theme, I've seen six ladders, rungs and feet intersecting, forming crazy-angled planes on which to prop books. Other ideas likely to inspire a double-take? Bookshelves made out of, er, books (using a cruciform metal connector); a bookcase incorporating a reading cave; one with a tiny open fire at one end; and – my personal favourite – shelves spelling the word 'READ'.

ABOVE LEFT Designed by Ron Arad in 1994, Kartell's wittily named 'Bookworm' is an extruded plastic shelf that can be formed into any desirable shape. Each support can bear up to 10 kg, and its form means that books can be positioned on both inside and outside curves.

ABOVE RIGHT The attention-seeking 'Bookworm' works best in conjunction with plain materials and white walls.

OPPOSITE FAR RIGHT This open storage unit for books has a winding, sculptural quality reminiscent of 'Bookworm' – and enlivens the dead space between doorways.

RIGHT Owned by the Mazouz brothers and fitted out by decorator Bambi Sloan, Derrière is an achingly trendy 'secret' restaurant in the Marais district of Paris – the fashion world's canteen du jour. Fitted out like a kooky apartment with chambers, the former sweatshop features an illegal smoker's speakeasy in the attic with crazily angled bookshelves and wonky hunting trophies lit by leaning wall sconces.

BELOW Given second prize at the Green Furniture Awards 2010, Amy Hunting's 'Blockshelf' uses 20 kinds of random untreated wood found in a timber importer's waste bin and two cotton ropes. Everything is held together by basic knots used in sailing.

trees, a yellow tower that zigzags its way to the ceiling, or a cluster of floating 'clouds' that each holds a few books. Some of these designs shade into art objects with dubious utility (I'm thinking of a leaning bookcase here – the 'Pisa') – not that that particularly matters if one has more straight-up-and-down shelving elsewhere. And in a fairly minimal interior, it must be said that a honeycomb of stretched white hexagons, a scrolling sheet of metal or a 'rolling' shelf made of pink polypropylene makes quite a statement.

BOOKS ON PARADE

Living rooms are also the places into which you welcome friends and family, and inevitably a stack of books will inspire scrutiny and comment. The

OPPOSITE Salvaged wooden boards – held together by metal stays top and bottom – form pillars of books beneath a massive beam in an Italian farmhouse. The unexpected elegance of Katrin Arens's design derives from the thinness of the recessed metal shelves, which won't sag because they each hold so few titles.

ABOVE It's rare to have to pay the underside of shelves much consideration – except when they are right by the ceiling, as here. Here old door panels have been tongue-and-grooved together to form a gently surreal substitute cornice: the proportions seem familiar, but because they are not upright and inside a lintel something appears awry.

term 'coffee-table book' used to be delivered with a sneer to imply the triumph of style over substance – but some subjects really do deserve to be picture-led (this one, for example!), and our increasing sophistication as a society with 'reading' imagery means that we're more discerning. A selection of glossy titles surrounded by seating is the perfect launchpad for conversation, whether you're dipping into a survey of graffiti art or an atlas of world religion.

One aspect of displaying one's collection that unites most bibliophiles in dread is 'borrowers of books – those mutilators of collections, spoilers of the symmetry of shelves, and creators of odd volumes'. So wrote the social ecologist Peter F. Drucker, but the sentiment is writ large. Part of the problem is that for a specific personality

type building a library is, as Rob Kaplan puts it, 'a means of taking possession'. Kaplan always writes the purchase date inside the cover of a new book, despite never later needing to know. By mortaring together these little bricks of information and wisdom one is constructing a fortress of rationality in a meaningless universe. The borrower wrecks this, for in truth what percentage of books that you lend do you ever get back? Bibliomane Roger Rosenblatt feels anxious when he sees a friend peering intently at his living-room shelves: 'the eyes, dark with calculation, shift from title to title as from floozie to floozie in an overheated dance hall'. We can thus sympathize with critic Anatole Broyard, who wrote: 'I feel about lending a book the way most fathers feel about their daughters living out of wedlock.'

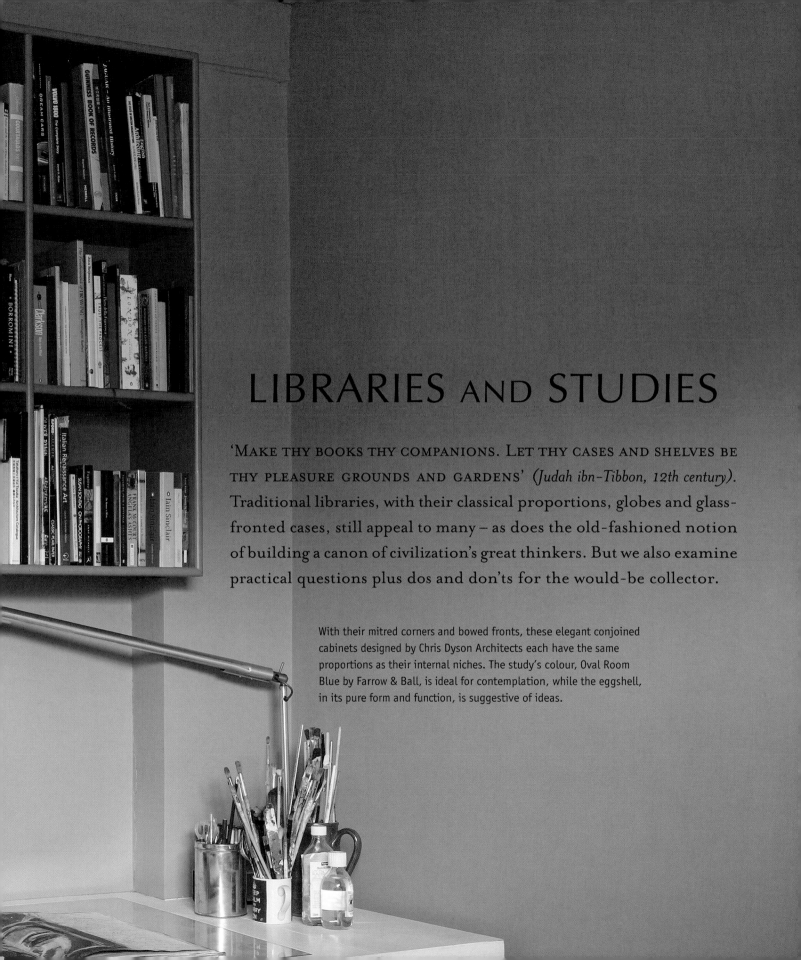

LIBRARIES AND STUDIES

'MAKE THY BOOKS THY COMPANIONS. LET THY CASES AND SHELVES BE THY PLEASURE GROUNDS AND GARDENS' *(Judah ibn–Tibbon, 12th century)*. Traditional libraries, with their classical proportions, globes and glass-fronted cases, still appeal to many – as does the old-fashioned notion of building a canon of civilization's great thinkers. But we also examine practical questions plus dos and don'ts for the would-be collector.

With their mitred corners and bowed fronts, these elegant conjoined cabinets designed by Chris Dyson Architects each have the same proportions as their internal niches. The study's colour, Oval Room Blue by Farrow & Ball, is ideal for contemplation, while the eggshell, in its pure form and function, is suggestive of ideas.

A private library represents not simply the sum total of books that someone has acquired through his or her life; rather, it characteristically mirrors and fleshes out a range of serious interests. In his essay 'Books Unread', the American preacher Thomas Wentworth Higginson writes about running out of shelf space and summoning his joiner. When the latter asked him: 'Have you actually read all these books?' he responded: 'Have you actually used all the tools in your tool box?' No – the key point is that he has them on hand in case he should need them. In this sense, the library is more a working tool, for consultation, than simply a storehouse of books read.

A WORLD OF WISDOM

There is always an aspirational element to library founders, the urge to capture the centuries of wisdom in paper form – what Umberto Eco has called 'vegetable memory'. In 1771, the 28-year-old Thomas Jefferson was asked by his future brother in-law, Robert Skipwith, to draw up a list of

OPPOSITE All manner of book storage, from an escritoire to wrought-iron bookends, has been pressed into service in this study in an ancient cottage. Despite the walls' thickness – meaning that books can be shelved two deep – a sheepskin rug is needed to keep the chill at bay.

RIGHT Although horizontals do not align, the bookshelves in this French antique dealer's library do echo the structure of a classical column. The dado rail and elements of the coving have been picked out in gold.

years ago by the outgoing president of Harvard University, Charles W. Eliot. He claimed that any person, reading just 15 minutes a day, could receive a good 'liberal education' by acquiring just 50 carefully selected volumes. The 'five-foot shelf' of Harvard Classics, as it came to be known, could be bought in one fell swoop and included works by the likes of Plato, Milton, Benjamin Franklin, Darwin, Dante, Adam Smith and Shakespeare (though it lacked scientific works, novels or any writing by women).

THE TRADITIONAL LIBRARY

The desire to surround oneself with the fruits of civilization has not entirely waned, and those with wealth at their disposal may well want to retain some, if not all, of the features of a formal library. This might typically be a double-height room – overlooked by a ceiling fresco of Apollo, goddess of wisdom – with the books on the upper level being reached via a wooden gallery with a staircase. Partly because ancient Greece and Rome have been regarded historically as the wellsprings of Western culture, traditional libraries have often been designed along classical lines. Floor-to-ceiling bookshelves typically have a vertical emphasis and consciously echo the structure of a column: the bottom third (often housing cupboards below dado level) juts further forward; uprights might be reeded, alluding to the fluted shafts of pillars; and shelves

ABOVE AND OPPOSITE
In 1939, poet laureate John Betjeman wrote approvingly of Tullynally Castle in County Westmeath, Ireland. The architect maintained the cubic character of its oak-panelled library by building the shelves into the thickness of the walls, with a wooden architrave flush to the line of the plaster. The jib door (*opposite*) means that the eye is not interrupted.

books 'suited to the capacity of the common reader who understands but little of the classicks and who has not leisure for intricate or tedious study'. The future third president of the USA's list included 148 titles, mostly classics, but with some practical works, such as Jethro Tull's *Horse Hoeing Husbandry*. The notion of a canon was further refined around 100

OPPOSITE One of the most impressive aspects of Deborah Bowness's 'Genuine Fake Bookshelf' wallpaper is that there are no repeats over the course of its 330cm drop. The sense of optical disorientation is here enhanced by the giant Anglepoise lamp.

RIGHT Leather- and buckram-bound books seem to demand shelves of a certain quality. These flange-fronted cases are deep enough to share space with elegant objects, such as miniature busts, dried gourds and wooden marquetry candlesticks.

get narrower towards the top. The entire ensemble might be topped off with a 'cornice', decorated with a frieze. Purpose-built libraries of this kind often have their shelves recessed into the walls.

Books bound in leather and buckram often have a uniform appearance, reflecting the fact that in the 18th and 19th centuries publishers in their current form didn't exist, and the wealthy had books bound themselves. Stacks might feature numeric and alphabetic codes, picked out in discreet gold leaf, that cross-refer to a card system showing where different items in the collection are housed. A large ornately carved study table would typically also incorporate a plan-chest element, with wide shallow drawers to store maps and engravings. Library steps and lecterns contribute to the whole process of access and consultation. Other decorative features of these formal spaces carry symbolic freight. Globes refer to the geographical spread of learning through trade and colonization, while plaster busts of men of genius, from Ben Franklin to Goethe, proclaim the fruits of the Enlightenment mission. Clocks allude to the fact that every epoch's intellectual achievements rest on those of previous ages – and there's a vanitas element too: so much to know, so little time.

BOOK SNOBS

Using the possession of books as a means to enhance your social status has a long pedigree. In the late 16th century, Louis Le Roy sneered at those who collected books 'well printed, bound and gilded, to serve only

PURPOSE-BUILT LIBRARIES OFTEN HAVE THEIR SHELVES RECESSED INTO THE WALLS

for ornaments, which they never look in themselves, nor suffer others, for fear of fouling them'. John Bunyan, writing a few decades later, is severe on 'the pride of a library' and those who 'take more pleasure in the number of, than the matter contained in, their books'. Today there are book snobs for whom owning a library, the more leather-bound the better, provides incomparable 'tone'. One website aimed at Americans sells dusty Danish- and German-language tomes by the yard in order to furnish an image. Faux

books – those hollow blocks of ersatz erudition – are also readily available, and surely ludicrous if the aim is self-aggrandisement. But I'm glad to discover that Dickens' study had a secret door designed to look like a bookcase; it featured fake works with witty titles, such as *Noah's Arkitecture* and a nine-volume set titled *Cats' Lives*. (Book wallpaper – such as Brunschwig and Fils's 'Bibliothèque' – is another light-hearted way to conceal a jib door, especially in a library or a nook.)

COLLECTING BOOKS: FIRST PRINCIPLES

Bibliomanes – and they may or may not be avid readers – can't stop hunting down books for their libraries. It is an itch that can never be scratched. As the Marxist writer Walter Benjamin saw it: 'The loss of a book can turn some people into invalids, and the desire to acquire one can turn others into criminals.' More balanced collectors might build a library around a core of interests. The novelist John Fowles collected travel books, old murder trials and historical memoirs; for him, these genres were like 'science fiction in reverse' – offering little time capsules of the periods they were written in. You might seek out works of a specific author, or subject, or binding style; or look to acquire a series. You may want to collect rare works by a well-known author or, say, paperbacks from the heyday of science fiction. Most guides to collecting advocate this principle: specialize or waste your money. Some other basic rules of thumbs are that a book's value is directly linked to market demand; that the condition of a book, and whether it possesses a dust jacket, is crucial to its value; that one should adopt a 'buy low, sell high' mentality by looking for books that have not yet shot up in value – the closer to the publication date the better.

Serious collectors will certainly use see-through plastic sleeves to protect collectable dust jackets

ABOVE These 19th-century oak library steps, complete with hand grips for extra security, are an essential accessory for the floor-to-ceiling library of an antique dealer in Uzès, in France. The signs of bibliophilia are evident in the lack of concern shown in matching up the horizontals and the desire to squeeze in as many volumes as possible: there is virtually no air above any of the head caps.

OPPOSITE Bookcases on runners are a rather more elegant solution to space constraints than the old stand-by of shelving one's collection two deep. Here, in the apartment of a New York architect, a featherweight paper light fitting contrasts with the imposing structure, while an original 'DCM' moulded-plywood dining chair by Eames reminds us of the joys of simpler engineering.

(often 60 per cent of a first edition's value) and may well consider installing glass-fronted cabinets to keep dust at bay. Ultraviolet radiation causes fading and deterioration of books, so keep direct sunlight at bay, diffusing it with louvres, blinds or slatted screens. Downlighters can be installed at the top of stacks, and these can be combined with more mobile clip-on lights. If you live in a region where the summers are baking and the winters freezing, you should consider controlling the temperature, and try to avoid placing shelves against an outside wall: thermal differences between inside and outside can lead to condensation building up in the pocket behind the shelves, which in turn can cause mould. Foxing, the unsightly reddish-brown spots that afflict ageing paper, is also thought to be caused by moisture in the air, so a well-placed dehumidifier is not a bad idea. Placing your books centrally (depthwise) on the shelves is also a good idea for helping air to circulate – and try to avoid either books leaning at angles or being too densely packed; both approaches will end up damaging the spines.

THE CONDITION OF A BOOK, AND WHETHER IT POSSESSES A DUST JACKET, IS CRUCIAL TO ITS VALUE

OPPOSITE A door in the library at Tullynally Castle, in County Westmeath, Ireland, leads to a turret. The first books here were acquired by Elizabeth Pakenham in the 1780s, later made First Countess of Longford, who presided over a Dublin salon described by one commentator as a place where 'one was always sure to meet the cleverest people in the county'. Evelyn Waugh admired the room greatly.

RIGHT Lack of pretension rules in the library of a writer, editor and academic in London. Instead of the classic library steps, Alvar Aalto's three-legged birch stool is used as a leg-up for books on the upper tiers – though it might be a stretch too far to reach the overspill titles unceremoniously plonked on top of the cabinets. Under the circumstances, one wonders why the curious mirrored central alcove was not used to house more, er, books.

OPPOSITE Organizing by publisher only makes sense in the context of particular series, such as Random House's 750-strong 'Modern Library', or a specialist house with a particular look, e.g. Virago's green-covered reprints of early 20th-century classics.

RIGHT With their distinctive logo and orange-and-white covers, Penguin paperbacks – the brainchild of Allen Lane – were the first of their kind, and look great gathered together.

FAR RIGHT To keep the price low, budget editions of the classics were often published in plain covers in the mid-20th century – and will never disrupt a minimalist scheme.

BELOW RIGHT The gilt-edged pages of a multi-volume encyclopedia add lustre to any bookcase.

ORGANIZING YOUR COLLECTION

In Anne Fadiman's charming essay 'Marrying Libraries', she points to the apparent incompatibility between her and her future husband's modus operandi: 'His books commingled democratically, united under the all-inclusive flag of Literature. Some were vertical, some horizontal, and some actually placed behind others. Mine were balkanized by nationality and subject matter.' Ultimately, her 'French garden' approach overcame his 'English garden' one.

The simple answer to this conundrum is… er, there is no simple blanket solution for one's whole collection, but the most common compromise is to divide one's books into genres (e.g. fiction, art, travel, science, design) and then organize alphabetically by author within those groups. Then again (if visual effect trumps accessibility), one can arrange strictly by size – as Samuel Pepys did in his famous library of 3,000 books – or by colour. An interesting variant is by publisher, especially those with visually distinctive covers, such as Granta or Gallimard. And what about these possibilities? By order of acquisition, by publication date, by the Dewey Decimal system… hey, it's your house!

LEFT Having face-out shelves, as here in events stylist Jo Berryman's study, is handy if you are working on a particular project and need to flit back and forth between different titles for valuable inspiration.

OPPOSITE This exceptionally solid tripartite bookcase matches the sofa's three divisions. Its soft leather, plus the low lighting and red walls, evokes the warm atmosphere of a gentleman's club, one conducive to quiet concentration.

STUDIES

A study does not require a library's worth of books, but the two spaces are certainly cousins. At their most refined, studies reveal a great deal about the occupant's attitude to organization, his enthusiasms and quirks of character. For here, in one's intellectual lair, personal foibles can be indulged. Eamonn McCabe's series of photographs, 'Writers' Rooms', captured the idiosyncrasies beautifully. So we discovered that Will Self has a chimneybreast in his study covered with a military-style grid of yellow stickers; that of Beryl Bainbridge, meanwhile, contained a model of the Titanic. While V. S. Naipaul's room is bare and characterless, the critic and poet Clive James works surrounded by chaos: 'There are books I know I own, but I have to buy them again because I can't find them.'

More of us are working from home. Rising overheads combined with the connectivity of technology mean that more companies are 'outsourcing'; the freelance life is on the up and up – and thus so too are home offices. They can

Something about the long views of a loft militates against focused work, which is why the owner of this one has tucked a home office with bookshelves behind a partial dividing wall. Cleverly, though, she has differentiated even this small area, installing a platform for lateral thinking on poufs up behind the desk area.

RIGHT In this New York apartment, architects Ogawa/Depardon show what you can do if you have to site your office in a murky space: a translucent yellow cotton screen glows with backlit sunshine, a globe and exotic travel posters evoke sweltering weather and the cunningly designed desk contains a secret stash of what looks like holiday reading when the prospect of real work palls.

ABOVE This improvised office in the Italian countryside makes full use of the vivid natural light by placing the desk in front of french windows, while the low-hanging pendant pools the light after dark. The corner location, moreover, means that both bookcases are within easy reach, and the drawers they contain mean that an old kitchen table (rather than a desk) will suffice.

range from a full-blown study to an old table with a shelf of reference books above it. They're often a dual-purpose space, sometimes doubling as a dining room or guest room. Shelving can be off the peg and functional, though often it's a signature piece (like a house plant, designer chair or flamboyant light) and distinctive belongings (photos, favourite objects) that make the impersonal elements recede. If a part of a larger room needs to be screened off to create an office away from the bustle of domestic life, it sometimes makes sense to use a shelving unit as a partition. Do not allow the space to be colonized by ranks of boring primary-coloured box files – at the very least, wrap them in decorative papers.

OPPOSITE Elegant tongue-and-groove panelling supports family photographs and pen-and-ink drawings, personalizing this study. Books in active use stack up at one end of the L-shaped desk, while an unusual 'floating' case houses the majority. Three uprights support the unit, and the upper two shelves are cantilevered out from a back section. Spot the semi-dividers, like built-in bookends.

OPPOSITE With nail holes along their weathered edges, these salvaged timbers have a rough-hewn quality offset by gauzy curtains and a pretty floral still life. The makeshift shelves are robust enough to hold a long line of hardbacks without sagging.

Graphic designers often gush about the virtues of white space on the page – and the same can apply to interiors. In this study in Provence, the empty spaces in the shelf cavities help make their contents – a wooden sailboat, an apothecary jar, a worn bucket and so on – stand out. The overall impression is artful but casual, even the visual rhyme of the handmade ladder with the table's trestles, and the fact that the laptop is also white.

KITCHENS AND DINING ROOMS

'SOME BOOKS ARE TO BE TASTED, OTHERS TO BE SWALLOWED, AND SOME FEW TO BE CHEWED AND DIGESTED' *(Francis Bacon)*. No room has changed more than the kitchen in the last thirty years. Its shift from site of drudgery to heart of the home has made cooking seem glamorous. This affects how and where we store our books – whether that space is a slick designer creation or one that would grace a farmhouse.

In this version of 'My Kitchen', designed by Modulnova, the books are sited well away from food preparation areas on a long low shelf perpendicular to a breakfast bar, making them handy for browsing. Since no element in this show kitchen is allowed to clash with white-gloss and black-matt-wave polymeric finishes, the books have been covered in greys, whites and blacks. Credit: Alternative Plans

Readers are consumers, and books food for the soul; we savour a writer's prose, have a taste for biography and live on a diet of mystery stories (even if they're half-baked). Carlo Petrini, who founded the Slow Food movement in the late 1980s to counter the spread of McDonalds in Italy, expressed his philosophy succinctly: 'When I wear a pair of Armani trousers they do not become part of me. When I eat a piece of ham it does. That's why I spend money on food.' Perhaps the same applies to books. Few people in the modern world get through a hard week at the office without indulging in the odd ready-meal while relaxing in front of some mindless telly. But it's not too much of a stretch to contrast the ping of a microwave and a half-hour of canned laughter, on the one hand, with a lovingly prepared casserole and the deeper satisfactions of a well-crafted novel, on the other.

CHANGES IN KITCHEN DESIGN

In the postwar period, when *Mrs Beeton's Book of Household Management* was still the housewife's trusty aid, the steam and smoke of kitchens meant that they were often sealed off from the other living spaces. They can seem like domestic prisons to modern eyes. Julian Barnes, in his essay 'The Late-Onset Cook', writes: 'Meals and my mother emerged from it – meals often based on my father's garden produce – but neither he, my brother, nor I enquired, or were encouraged to enquire, about the transformational process.' The perfecting of extractor fans in the 1980s was an important factor in enabling the kitchen to become more open-plan. Dining and food-preparation areas often became umbilically linked, and the farmhouse kitchen became fashionable, even in urban areas. This reintegration of cooking with other living areas changed the perception of food preparation into a skilled, creative and even status-conscious activity. The

classic 'trophy kitchen', filled with expensive (and often little-used) gadgets, shows how culinary accomplishment has become worth advertising; and likewise celebrity chefs exploit public perceptions of their desirable lifestyles to help sell their glossy recipe books.

RECIPES OF A LIFETIME

Taste and smell are the senses that are like a hotline to your past. Famously, in Proust's *Remembrance of Things Past*, dipping a madeleine in lime-blossom tea immediately sets off a train of memories within the

OPPOSITE This sleek storage unit (which also doubles as a space to hold electric cables and switches) acts as a transition between living and cooking zones. The shelves assert themselves not only by offering a hot hue in a sea of cool blue but by protruding from their surround by several centimetres.

It is fairly common in Victorian houses for the basement area to be converted into one large space with a kitchen near the garden and a large dining area – once the servants' quarters – beyond. The chimneybreast and alcoves replicate the arrangement on the ground floor above.

BELOW In this slick kitchen available from Alternative Plans, slender dark-oak-veneer open units containing books are interspersed with cabinets fronted with a noisette glossy glass. With the breakfast bar running at right angles, the cookbooks are ideally placed for browsing.

narrator. Similarly, the cookbooks that you keep in your kitchen are not merely repositories of recipes, but reminders of adult rites of passage: shared student digs, the move to a bachelor pad, settled coupledom. And unless you're the kind of person that protects their cookbooks behind Perspex, every stain tells a story, reminding one of romantic trysts, raucous dinner parties and fraught family lunches. Breaking bread may bring people together, but in the 21st century this attachment to the centrality of shared meals sounds increasingly romantic. According to a recent survey by a leading insurance company, only one in ten of us has time for breakfast round the kitchen table and only one in three households

BELOW In this Copenhagen kitchen, the monochrome scheme is lightened by decorative touches, from the Neo-Nouveau pendant to the Betty Boop cut-out. The long sweep of the table, with its Jacobsen 'Butterfly' chairs, is emphasized by the 'floating' black shelves and horizontal stacks of books.

sits down to an evening meal together. In fact there has been a shift in the last 30 years that's seen kitchens turn from being utilitarian galleys to multifunctional hubs of the home, where we study, chat with our housemates or catch up on our emails. This affects where and how we store our books, and what books they are.

FITTED KITCHENS

Apart from the single-file galley, most modern kitchen design is predicated on the idea of a work triangle formed from the three functions of storage, preparation and cooking, with, say, the refrigerator, sink and cooker as the three vertices. When

In this Philadelphia home, bookshelves on brackets display an informal and unpretentious practicality. Even in this relaxed set-up, the books on the lower levels lie sideways, while upper occupants stand vertical, echoing the plinth-like structure of a classical column.

BELOW Stylist Anja Koops and chef Alain Parry have wittily cannibalized the horns of a small goat or deer to serve as a cookbook stand in their Amsterdam home – the ideal gizmo for a trophy kitchen, perhaps.

RIGHT Contraform's 'Quad' has so many different-sized apertures that you can use it to store a wide variety of different items, not just books. It makes a nice contrast to the flush rectilinearity of most modern unit kitchens.

considering how to store your books, bear in mind that these areas should be reasonably close together and that ease of circulation should be optimized, with as few obstacles as possible. However many cookbooks you own, most people have a core of much-loved, familiar stalwarts to which they turn time and time again. If space is at a premium, other broader-brush titles such as food encyclopedias or cuisine from a specific region can be stored elsewhere and brought in to play on an ad hoc basis.

Any fitted kitchen that you buy, however cheap, will these days be custom-designed, so make sure you allocate space to house not only these 'capsule' cookbooks but also the loose-leaf folders of passed-down family favourites and enticing clippings from newspapers and magazines; these can also be stored on shelves in pretty boxes or wicker baskets.

People who are worried about keeping their cookbooks pristine can consider putting them behind glass or cupboard doors. On balance, however, modern kitchens can look too much like hygienic

Charlotte Gueneau, co-founder of Danish interiors company Rice, has stopped her two short shelves looking isolated by matching their length and thickness to the wooden tabletop beneath. Supported by brackets hidden under plaster, they appear to float gracefully.

RIGHT A wooden shelf with brackets is classic farmhouse kitchen territory, particularly when it sits above cream earthenware tiles, an old-fashioned weighing scale and a crystal cake stand.

FAR RIGHT Higgledy-piggledy arrangements are all part of the charm of old-fashioned kitchens, and this weathered piece of furniture doubles as a shelf for supporting containers and books, and a rack for mugs.

BELOW You might not want your regular cookbooks stored in this relatively inaccessible spot, tucked up against the supporting pillar and beam of this open-plan Victorian kitchen, but it would be ideal for the kind of food reference books dipped into occasionally.

BOOKS ON SHOW ADD PERSONALITY AND A WASH OF COLOUR

laboratories. Books on show add personality and a wash of colour to a monochrome space – and serve as physical reminders that the enjoyable work of preparing food speaks more to human fundamentals than parading hip electrical brands. That said, in sleek unit kitchens, the flowing lines of worktops and flush units are emphasized by keeping all extraneous clutter stored beneath or above until ready for use. It looks good to recess shelves into a stud wall, so that spines do not jut out into the space, thereby interrupting sightlines. Make sure, too, that bookshelves built into the corner of a fitted kitchen have enough depth, so that larger format titles do not stick out, interfering with drawers and doors at a right angle. Upper cabinets are hung on one level such that their handles can be reached easily by adults; in a high-ceilinged kitchen this may leave ample room to store books on top of them – though this will add considerable weight to units already crammed with

ABOVE The sage and muted-yellow tongue-and-groove cupboards and walls make a memorable contrast with the luxurious sheen of the stainless-steel worktop and fridge, while the little rectangular orange cabinet pulls everything together. The panelling combines with the cutlery rack to create a strongly rhythmical vertical stress – perhaps too much so for the owner, who has left her cookbooks askew.

crockery, glasses and foodstuffs, so check they are very securely fastened to the walls. In larger open-plan spaces, there are two other options: islands – either central worktops or larger breakfast bars – make great spaces to store your cookbooks; they are both efficiently tucked away but swiftly accessible. And where kitchen and sitting areas are all in one, an open shelving unit can partially screen the space – when guests are around, this can allow the cook to concentrate on the tasks at hand, but also the chance to chat during lulls.

FARMHOUSE KITCHENS

In a typical farmhouse kitchen, the mechanics of food preparation are more likely to be on show. Instead of ranks of identikit units with doors, crockery is likely to

be displayed on a dresser, pots hang from hooks and cookbooks – the more well-thumbed the better – might have a dedicated shelf made, say, of pine with rustic brackets. These kinds of kitchens offer sociability. Traditionally, they benefit from the heat of an Aga and are painted in cosy reds and creams, but the warmth also derives from the mix-and-match nature of the furniture on display, a solid wooden table feeling like a natural extension of the cooking area. A little case of books nearby, or a shelf run beneath a window seat overlooking the vegetable patch, encourages people to gravitate to this womb-like space; it also allows the chef to pause while a pie bakes or a stock burbles, have a slug of sherry and lose himself briefly in a book. Given that these kitchens often lead directly to a garden, this is also a handy spot for horticultural guides.

ABOVE CENTRE From the antique rolling pin hanging by a loop of string to the pretty dinner service, everything here has been lovingly worn by use. Open-ended shelves employ a little pile to serve as an impromptu bookend.

ABOVE RIGHT Although the central space on a dresser is traditionally occupied by mugs on hooks, it can also be used as a snug cavity for books.

DINING ROOMS

Just as 'dressing for dinner' now sounds like an anachronism, the enclosed dining room (complete with sideboard holding china for special occasions and topped with a carriage clock) may also be fading, along with the formality that accompanies it. Even if a household possesses the luxury of a separate dining room, its members tend to eat most of the time at the kitchen table, or indeed with their plates on their laps in front of the TV. To save it from being

OPPOSITE As soon as books are placed behind glass doors the attention is diverted to the furniture that encases them. That's no bad thing in a dining room, where serried ranks of books can sit ill with the earthy activity of feeding. Here in the 16th-century Somerset home of a garden designer, one suspects this cabinet is bespoke, it fits the space so perfectly. The rough-hewn wooden utensils and clay vessels above act as a warmly human counterpoint to its cool shade and clean lines.

ABOVE In this rather murky dining room in an antique dealer's house in France, light is reflected back into the room by the glass-fronted cabinet rather than being absorbed by books. The gothic beading that articulates the panes finds a visual echo in the charming provincial scrollwork chandelier, from which hang metal stars, crystal drops and golden finials. Although, overall, the effect is overwhelmingly neutral, the knots in the table and hessian on the chairs add texture, and the spines add discreet colour.

hugely under-exploited on a day-to-day basis, the dining room often doubles as a working area or library, in part because there's already a large table on hand. Books work well here anyway, because they are convivial mealtime companions – to occupy the solitary diner, to spark off dinner-party banter or to settle family disputes on special occasions. All that cloth, leather and paper muffles the clink of glasses and the clatter of cutlery on plates. Try to match the style (and even thickness) of bookshelves to the table, and you can hang small pictures from some of the uprights to stop the atmosphere becoming indigestibly intellectual.

THIS PAGE AND OPPOSITE
Interior designer Paul Daly
custom-designed this modular
'floating' storage system for
an apartment in the Barbican.
The mix of open and closed
cabinets means that storage
of dining-room necessaries
(cruets, china, placemats) can
be combined with the display
of books and CDs. The carefully
aligned tower of books on the
floor offers, along with the steel
lamp, a vertical contrast to
the overwhelmingly horizontal
emphasis of the units.

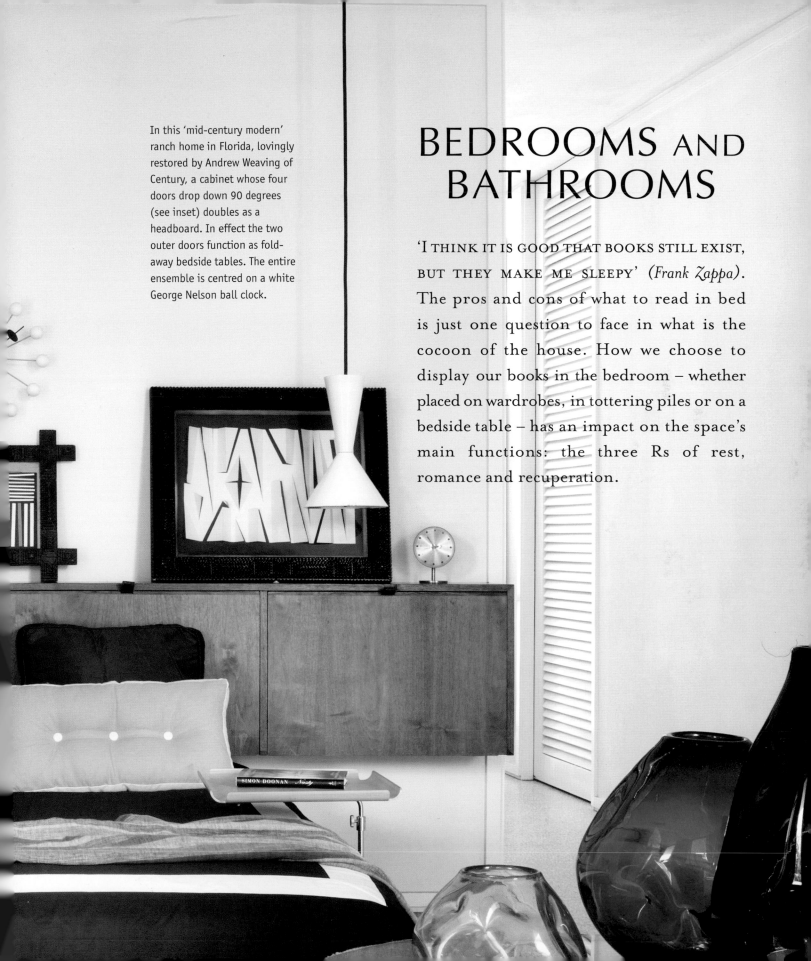

In this 'mid-century modern' ranch home in Florida, lovingly restored by Andrew Weaving of Century, a cabinet whose four doors drop down 90 degrees (see inset) doubles as a headboard. In effect the two outer doors function as fold-away bedside tables. The entire ensemble is centred on a white George Nelson ball clock.

BEDROOMS AND BATHROOMS

'I THINK IT IS GOOD THAT BOOKS STILL EXIST, BUT THEY MAKE ME SLEEPY' (*Frank Zappa*). The pros and cons of what to read in bed is just one question to face in what is the cocoon of the house. How we choose to display our books in the bedroom – whether placed on wardrobes, in tottering piles or on a bedside table – has an impact on the space's main functions: the three Rs of rest, romance and recuperation.

In an ideal world, bedrooms would be devoted solely to sleep, serenity and sex; décor suggestive of relaxation and intimacy would attempt to match the mood. People rarely do live in an ideal world however: bedrooms are often where people stash their clutter away from the eyes of visitors, whether it's payslips in a box under the bed or rolls of wrapping paper down the side of the wardrobe. Mess, it must be said, is far from restful. Similarly, many people, especially in cities, live in houses that feel short of a room or two; to escape the hurly-burly of communal spaces they often have little option sometimes but to retreat upstairs if they want to compose emails, talk on the phone, listen to music or study.

The cocoon-like nature of the bedroom may actually encourage concentration; many writers have thought so. John Updike noted that Proust, Colette and Edith Wharton all scribbled away under the blankets, while James Joyce 'sprawled across his and Nora's bed in a riot of notes to himself'. The asthmatic Proust lined his precisely arranged bedroom in his Paris apartment with cork tiles, shutting out the noise and dust of Boulevard Haussmann. Sleeping by day and working by night, he completed *Remembrance of Things Past*

OPPOSITE Take a bateau-lit bed, a black-and-white snap of the beach, a column of battered leather suitcases – complete with vintage stickers – and an old dial telephone, and one wonders which little pile of books you'll be ploughing through on the deck of an Art Deco ocean liner.

LEFT This tall, elegant recess is part of a bed surround in an Arts and Crafts house in Wales, a commissioned copy of Charles Rennie Mackintosh's Hill House near Glasgow.

RIGHT ABOVE A simple wrought-iron bracket serves as a prop for bedside reading.

RIGHT In this Italian house, rustic furniture by Katrin Arens contrasts with Artemide's beautifully engineered 'Tolomeo' mini wall lamp.

THIS PAGE AND OPPOSITE
Well I never – a pile of books
supporting a bookshelf!
Actually, it's a drawer filled
with the jewellery of artist and
craftsman Nathalie Lété in
Paris. The festooned necklaces,
hand-sewn hearts and quirky
appliqués above the bed head
add up to a romantic, intensely
personal cocoon of a bedroom.

by treating the room as a storehouse of memories and a shield against the outside world. Unfortunately, the focus required to marshal one's thoughts and get the brain's synapses firing is inimical to falling asleep afterwards. Psychologists who treat insomniacs advise against combining a work/study area with a bedroom, but beggars do not always get to choose.

One compromise is to keep one's desk, laptop and shelf of reference books in a specific zone, visually separate from where you wind down.

READING IN BED

It is a different matter when it comes to reading for pleasure. The novel is ideal for the bedroom; it's

This bracketed shelf running just above the pillows serves as a kind of headboard, with the photograph in the centre serving as a boundary marker between the books of the left-hand sleeper and those of his or her partner.

OPPOSITE Panel doors with invisible flush catches enclose a recessed bookshelf in this storage space above a bed. Downlighters in the underside of the units illuminate the headboard, which doubles as a shelf for family photographs, and the red upright telephone complements the grassy-green wall behind.

an inherently intimate form, in which we are given privileged access to the interior feelings of fictional characters. There's an emotional logic in gathering them about us in the one room where we are likely to withdraw to brood, plot a courtship or make plans to change one's life for the better. Harold Brodkey has compared immersing oneself in a good book to a love affair – also a pregnancy, for 'one is inside the experience and is about to be born'. A century earlier, Ralph Waldo Emerson wrote of 'books which rank in our life with parents and lovers and passionate experiences, so medicinal, so stringent, so revolutionary, so authoritative'.

In the witty essay 'Pillow Books', the *New Yorker*'s books editor, Clifton Fadiman, outlines two schools of thought when it comes to pre-slumber reading: books to keep you awake and books to get your head nodding. Though he mentions that Coleridge would

HAROLD BRODKEY HAS COMPARED IMMERSING ONESELF IN A GOOD BOOK TO A LOVE AFFAIR

LEFT A slab of wood affixed to elegant built-in wardrobes serves to both frame the doorway and prop up the box-like bookcase above the bedroom entrance. The rectangular volume is divided into two near halves, matching the proportions of the uppermost door panels. The little gap at the top, while of limited practical value for storage, has a deep shadow that reminds one of the full volume of the room.

read the blank-verse odes of his friend Southey when laudanum failed to help him lose consciousness, boring books generally make a poor opiate: 'dull books soothe only dull brains – a moderately healthy mind will be irritated rather than rested by a dull book'. On the other hand, one should avoid prose that provokes extreme responses, such as heart-thumping adventure yarns, side-splitting comedies or biographies of hated politicians – the kind of works about which Dorothy Parker said should 'not be tossed aside lightly' but 'thrown with great force'.

A 'Garden Gnome' (table) by
Philippe Starck smiles
approvingly at this pleasing
storage solution in a
Connecticut attic bedroom.
A long line of wall-to-wall
cupboards creates a platform
for books, which is visually
enclosed by the base of the
eaves strut. Because the room
is tucked up in the A-frame of
the roof, little wall space is
free for conventional shelves.

Reading books about travel might be problematic if you're feeling tethered or aching with wanderlust; likewise, books about food history or the cuisine of a particular region carry the attendant hazard of inspiring a trip to the fridge for a midnight feast. Last thing at night, reading should be 'a kind of small private devotion during which we beat a quiet retreat from the practical', bridging wakefulness and dreams. The best bedtime books, Fadiman concludes, are those that 'deny the existence of tomorrow'.

SHELVING ISSUES

How, then, should we store and display books in the bedroom? Well, Ella Berthoud, bibliotherapist at the School of Life in London, advises people to avoid keeping them there at all, 'apart from the one they're reading – because this space should be kept calm'. I disagree. Having at least your 'desert island' books around you – those you might regard as identity-forming – means you can enjoy your solitude while surrounding yourself with these undemanding old friends (unlike real friends, as Proust pointed out, when a book bores us we do not have to feign interest). One should

In this unusually shaped bedroom, the fact that two walls meet at an obtuse angle means that the problem of dealing with shelves that come together at 90 degrees doesn't need to be faced. The height of the door has necessitated one shelf with low clearance, which is why those novels are lying on their side.

ABOVE This cave-like bedroom under the eaves of an isolated Sussex cottage is rendered less stark by the romantic curves of its wrought-iron bed and the pretty patchwork quilt. The simple shelf brackets are masked by the existing timbers.

ABOVE RIGHT Light is admitted into this closeted bed in Castle Dodard, Ireland, via a panel that opens to the bright chamber beyond, making for a delightful reading spot. Modern restored and extended walls are covered with old maps to help them blend in.

certainly not feel oppressed by a whole wall of spines. If cosiness is your aim, then little stacks – tottering or rectilinear according to taste – are inviting, whether on a bedside table or ottoman, a bench at the foot of the bed, or even draped over the treads of a vintage ladder. You might be forced to go down this path if you are berthed under the eaves or in a converted attic with sloping walls.

In a smallish room, where the bed takes up much of the floor space, it's a nice idea to have a single shelf running high up near to the ceiling on three sides. Not only does it free up limited wall space, but you can also reach the otherwise inaccessible from the platform of your bed. And it even looks good, for such a shelf – especially if wooden and painted to contrast subtly with the colour scheme of the walls – serves as a substitute cornice, breaking up the rectilinearity of a boxy room. Other spaces that you can exploit while avoiding clutter are the gaps between sash windows and the tops of built-in wardrobes.

What greater encouragement to spend the morning in your bunk reading than to have shelves of books practically falling on to the pillow?

OPPOSITE A skylight is a reader's delight. The simple bracketed shelves, easily accessible from the platform created by the bed, fill the width of the wall but do not cramp the space. In this tiny box room, more storage space has been engineered under the mattress.

If your shelves are not full, keep books upright with either a bookend or with some object such as a vase (*opposite, above right*). Failing that, it is far better to stack your books horizontally (*above left*) than to allow them to lean, which puts undue pressure on spines. Another no-no is splaying open a book instead of using a bookmark: Persephone's grey editions have patterned bookmarks which match the endpapers (*opposite, below left*). Meanwhile, books in recessed walls should be insulated against thermal changes (*opposite, above left*).

CARING FOR YOUR BOOKS

First, let me swiftly deliver three dos and don'ts on daily handling. Make sure books are supported by bookends or their neighbours – never allow them to lean. At the same time, never access your books by grabbing the top of the spine, as the head cap will get damaged. And before making contact at all, wash your hands: most of the dirt on covers and pages is the accumulated grime of oily fingertips. For longer-term care, shield your books from unnecessary light and aim to clean them twice a year using a soft-bristled brush: work away from the spine, or the dust will be trapped there forever. This is a good chance to check for bookworms and moths. Though anointing the leather bindings of old books with creams is now frowned on, do take special care of their often-brittle structures by supporting with rolled-up towels on both sides. Finally, avoid storing your books for long periods in plastic (which can release dangerous gases) and do not banish them to attics or basements, which are subject to major fluctuations of temperature.

Shades of cream and white –
from the pale shells on the
chest of drawers to the snowy
slipcover on the armchair –
make for a restful reading
corner inside this latched
bedroom door. The concept has
even been extended to the
muted shades of the spines.

SHARING THE SHELVES

Up until now I have been writing for singletons, kings and queens of their own private domain. Other issues come into play when you are sharing the space with a spouse or partner. Most people are surprisingly territorial about which side of the bed they prefer, meaning that the time-honoured tradition of housing one's ongoing reading in bedside tables, left and right, works perfectly well. The presence of a double bed also throws

In this all-white bedroom, the upper partition helps to keep the book storage, cupboard and plants discrete from the bed area, which has been designated for sleep and sleep alone. The decorative effects of the chandelier and the curving wrought-iron chair keep blandness at bay.

up other design possibilities. One can have a long rectangular headboard that incorporates both space for books and built-in reading lights. Books in a headboard can also be backlit, creating a massif of silhouetted blocks; such an effect is visually soothing – bad for reading the spines, but then titles that close are those actively under consideration or being read. If your beloved is in complete harmony with your body clock, then you're lucky. Otherwise, night owls and early birds can sidestep a common source of domestic strife by carefully considering

THE GENRE OF LITERATURE SHOULD BE COMMENSURATE WITH THE LENGTH OF THE STAY

OPPOSITE Robert Levithan is a psychotherapist who has added interior design as a string to his bow. In this tiny New York apartment, his L-shaped solution squeezes in a lot of books, while allowing one to have an 'active' reading 'short list' immediately visible from the pillow area.

ABOVE RIGHT In what is a light-filled bedroom, with floor-to-ceiling windows, these glass-fronted barrister bookcases will help to deflect some of the sun's harmful rays while keeping dust at bay.

their night-time lighting needs; look into good cordless reading lights and LED book-clip lights – though the latter can be distracting to the reader.

BOOKS FOR GUESTS

If you have a guest staying, a discreet but always welcome piece of hospitality is to compile a judicious selection of books based on what you know – or, better, can intuit – about their tastes and enthusiasms. For the restless spirit, say, how about a photography book of the world's best free climbs, George Orwell's *Homage*

to Catalonia and *The Journals of Captain Cook*. For the scientist, try the essays of Stephen Jay Gould and Oliver Sacks's *The Man who Mistook His Wife for a Hat*. You get the idea. Needless to say, the genre of literature should be commensurate with the length of the stay – so essays, letters, short stories are good; chunky rip-roaring thrillers – especially if you'd like to see something of your visitor – less so. Whatever you opt for, most people who find a custom-designed library by their bedside will be bowled over by their hosts' thoughtfulness.

LOOS AND BATHROOMS

Likewise, when weighing up the ideal book for the loo, consideration of literary form is vital. Pithy quotations, *New Yorker* cartoons and verse anthologies (Seamus Heaney and Ted Hughes's *The Rattle Bag* is my favourite) are just right for that mood of peace and abstracted contemplation that comes upon men – it does seem to be mostly men – while in session. If you box in the cistern with attractive tongue-and-groove panelling, say, you create a ready-made shelf ideal for housing all those

ephemeral gift books that desperate people suddenly find themselves buying just before Christmas. And if the loo roll suddenly runs out… American novelist Henry Miller combined his lower functions with higher-brow tastes: 'There are passages of *Ulysses* which can be read only in the toilet – if one wants to extract the full flavor of their content.'

Humidity is a great foe of books, not only liquefying the glue that reinforces paperbacks' sewn signatures but also turning pages mouldy if allowed to fester. That's why, even allowing for extractor fans, any books stored in bathrooms should be behind doors or glass. That said, the steaminess created by a hot tub clears the respiratory tubes and lends itself to lucidity and lateral thinking. Napoleon spent two hours in a bath every morning girding himself for the day while an assistant read him newspapers and telegrams. The combination of privacy and ritual afforded by a good soak offers a break from life's stresses and strains. George Orwell, rarely regarded as frivolous, enjoyed leafing through his quirky collection of ladies' magazines from the 1860s while immersed. For those concerned about excessive moisture, you can buy metal book-rests specially designed for the bath.

FAR LEFT Just out of picture, a door can be shut on these neatly recessed shelves, offering some protection against humidity when the bath or shower is running.

LEFT This little square pocket of space above the loo-roll holder seems to cry out for a slim volume of haiku, Wildean epigrams or Doonesbury cartoons on its slender glass shelves. Why waste a moment of one's day when one could be enriching one's mind?

These chunky shelves in a narrow bathroom alcove are reminiscent of diving boards at different elevations – not a wholly inappropriate metaphor given the roomy lion's-foot bath beneath them. Although it's inadvisable to store books of any great value in a bathroom because of the steam, this one has high ceilings and plenty of ventilation. The radio on the gnarled olive-wood shelf by the tub completes the entertainment package.

STAIRS AND CORRIDORS

'He inched his way up the passageway as if he would rather be yarding his way down it...' *(Douglas Adams)* Corridors, staircases and landings are the in-between zones in the home. Often overlooked, they are crucial for aiding circulation and easing the transition between rooms with different functions, moods and décor. Artful lighting, ingenious shelving and the creation of reading nooks can turn these dead spaces into places worth lingering in.

A landing near the top of the house has been adapted to incorporate a low closet and a recess for books deep enough to house them two or three deep. The all-white surfaces bounce sunshine from the skylight into the dark corners.

INSET Across the stairs from a row of archetypal solids, we see that the bookshelves are supported not only by breezeblocks at each end, but by horizontal piles underneath. Without them, the shelves would be too slender for their burden.

A cartoon by Sam Gross, which appeared in a 1967 issue of the *New Yorker* magazine, shows a gangster and his fur-coated wife being shown round an empty house. Every visible wall is covered head to foot with empty bookshelves. She turns to the real-estate agent: 'Holy cow! What kind of crazy people used to live here anyway?' When the number of books you own starts creeping into the thousands, you basically have three options: a) implement a one-in, one-out policy; b) buy a bigger house; or c) look for ever more ingenious solutions to house your collection. The first two strategies are generally too painful to the psyche and the bank balance, respectively. Of course, for some bibliomanes, the lust to acquire will always outstrip the ability to shelve. Henry Petroski quotes the widow of one New York collector, whose 18-room apartment 'was so crowded with books that her step-children had to walk sideways down the hall to get to their (book-lined) bedrooms'. For those not quite that far gone, this chapter explores the slivers of real estate that connect the main

OPPOSITE The crude but effective construction of this book-lined ladder staircase – too short to do its job without a couple of extra bricks mortared together beneath – only enhances the rough-and-ready charm of this Sussex cottage.

RIGHT If you have recessed shelves that stop at the skirting of the stairs – rather than at the L-shaped steps themselves – the ends will terminate at a 45-degree angle. How did this sculptor in County Cork solve the problem? He didn't.

living areas of the house – hallways, corridors, staircases and landings – all of which are ripe for bookish exploitation.

STAIRCASES

The space underneath a staircase makes the ideal spot for a built-in ziggurat-style shelving unit – either filling the whole space, or as one section of a compact home office. A flight pointing in one direction is the most straightforward arrangement, of course, but even stairs that, say, turn down through 90 degrees to a basement area can, with ingenious carpentry, offer the space for a surprising number of books. Here we are speaking about converting an existing arrangement, but when putting in stairs from scratch, there are numerous more innovative set-ups. One visually impressive look is to have every other banister descending to form the uprights of the bookcase beneath. Another effective solution when the stairs bisect a space is to make them into a series of open-ended boxes that cascade upwards. While plenty of storage is offered, hollow cavities allow penetration of light.

Given the L-shaped nature of stairs, people with a serious overflow of books will be tempted to stack them left and right, leaving a narrow central path to get up and down. You need to have sufficient width so that, say, ten volumes can go on each tread without hampering passage. Undeniably, it's the kind of arrangement that would have a health-and-safety officer rolling his eyes, though one can minimize the dangers by securing the little clusters with the kind of slender metal bookends that can be partially hidden by a runner. Would it be facetious to suggest this as the ideal spot to store one's hiking and mountaineering titles? A neater solution, depending on the depth of your stairs (and your wallet), is to fashion drawers from the steps, openable with push fronts. With a very steep staircase, the kind that leads

THIS ARRANGEMENT WOULD HAVE A HEALTH-AND-SAFETY OFFICER ROLLING HIS EYES

ABOVE LEFT Seeing this tiny flat, the phrase 'a quart into a pint pot' comes to mind. It's always wise to check that a ladder staircase like this can support 400-odd books.

ABOVE AND OPPOSITE Levitate's ingenious 'library staircase', which accesses a new loft bedroom, holds up to 2,000 books in between its English oak treads.

This relocated staircase now climbs perpendicular to one of the alcoves formed by a basement chimneybreast. A delightful reading nook (enclosing extra storage beneath the mattress) is formed by the triangular volume under the stairs, whose wire banister allows light to penetrate from the storey above.

The chicken-wire grilles add an air of mystery in this pristine corridor. If the cupboards had solid doors, the overall effect would be uniformly clinical, and if they were open-fronted the riot of spines would upset the controlled minimalism. Thus the semi-opaque hint of hidden treasure strikes the right balance.

OPPOSITE Treasured family heirlooms, evidently well-thumbed, make a welcoming frame for a curtained dining-room doorway. In a busy household, this spot would fail as a reading nook, as it's in the swim of a circulation space – but it's actually the compact home of a singleton designer.

RIGHT This quietly dramatic reading space is reminiscent of a chamber in an ancient Roman villa, a connection emphasized by the classical plaster head lying on the day-bed shelf. The two towers of books seem to want to repel invaders, although the long perspectives in the enlarged photographs stop this nook feeling too cave-like.

NOOKS

If you share your house with others, reading a book in communal living areas can be a disturbing experience, and lying on one's bed can result in unwelcome drowsiness. Far better to set up a reading nook away from the hurly-burly, on a landing, in a passageway alcove or, in summer, in a hammock under a shady tree. Indoors, try to have at least two light sources, one natural, one artificial – the latter should ideally have a two- or three-way bulb that can be adjusted in wattage. A comfortable chair (perhaps with accompanying ottoman) is essential, and there's a range of interesting designer options that combine seating with book storage: two nice examples are Nobody & Co's 'Bibliochaise' (see page 39) and Pucci de Rossi's hollow rocking chair, the 'Dondola'. To assign a designated area for your child makes him or her feel special and can be a great spur to reading. Finally, add the stamp of personal eccentricity to your nook by gathering together the odd topics that show off your quirks – old children's annuals, Michelin guides, books about cars or paleontology or birds or... words.

LEFT These limed-oak bookcases, which connect a library to the sitting room beyond, manage to be both grand and relaxed at the same time, as befits a large home in rural Italy. The square portal, which frames an 18th-century mantelpiece, is supported by abstracted classical columns dividing into base, shaft and capital. The four carefully positioned standard lamps indicate what a serious pursuit reading is here.

RIGHT In this bibliophile's apartment, the floor-to-ceiling shelves in this passageway (leading to more of the same in the living area) would be overbearing were it not broken up by pools and shafts of light created by sconces and windows, respectively.

up to an attic space, it is even possible to form a bookcase enclosed on three sides, with the books stored in hollow risers and with cantilevered shelf-like stairs that double as perches from which to browse.

CORRIDORS

The trend these days is to see corridors as wasted space, but doing away with them to create a more open plan may, paradoxically, make one's living area seem smaller. Why? Because corridors offer architectural breathers, allowing us to imagine the space beyond; they are transitional zones that facilitate changes of mood – to help one smooth the shift from, say, grand to cosy. They are associated with intrigue: any mystery story worth its salt will have a false book that, when manipulated, activates a door to a secret passage. Moreover, because they are areas we pass through (rather than spend time in), we can actually be more adventurous in our décor; resist, above all, the temptation to use them as dumping grounds for things unwanted elsewhere.

Books placed out of reach are inevitably more enticing than those close to hand. The unusual shelf running across the tongue-and-groove ceiling has actually been designed to disguise an unsightly steel girder. The recess above the half-open door holds vintage mixing bowls.

OPPOSITE The long repeating lines of floorboards and bookshelves mean that the eye can easily be foxed by a strategically placed mirror. This one, concealing the entrance to a bedroom, turns a utilitarian passage into a slightly surreal scene from *Alice in Wonderland*.

NARROW-BEAMED DOWNLIGHTERS CREATE POOLS ALONG THE STRIP

Corridors make great spaces for storing books, but try to avoid a single monolithic wall of shelving – or at least try to make it take up no more than a third the height of the wall; circulation should never be hindered in traffic areas, and it is visually tedious to have a long thin space meandering endlessly on. Instead try to break up the space by interspersing bookcases with pictures, slender tables topped by vases, and mirrors – the decorator Jane Churchill recommends using outsize ones in tight spaces such as landings and corridors to dramatically reconfigure the space. Offer further contrast by using narrow-beamed downlighters to create pools along the strip, rather than a bland overall light. Cabinets that mix open shelving with closeted areas, and books with other objects, also militate against monotomy and claustrophobia. One can even have lights emanating from the shelves, either backlighting the volumes to create interesting abstract outlines, or behind coloured panels of glass to create a focal point.

What kind of books should one have in these spaces and how should they be organized? Since passageways are transitional spaces, it might make

sense to gather one's travel books here; a family of topics, from self-help to philosophy – the kind gathered together in bookshops under Mind, Body, Spirit – also suggests journeys, albeit of a more metaphorical kind. If ever there was a case for arranging books strictly by size, corridors – where one is trying to minimize visual clutter – might be the spot. It may be obvious, but the books you place high up in stairwells, above a cornice or running below a dado in a corridor should ideally be ones that you are not in the habit of consulting regularly.

HALLWAYS

Hallways make an important first impression to visitors, and if yours is already a riot of coats and shoes, adding bookcases, even high up the wall, will simply compound the sense of being hemmed-in. As a guest one wants to feel both welcomed and curious about what comes next. In a double-fronted property, in which the living areas are laid out to the left and right of the front door, there are more options because of the greater width. Instead of a traditional console table, one can position a bookcase beneath a ledge, dotted with objects, that projects out and therefore 'contains' the books beneath. If two doors face one another in the entrance area, there is nothing more dramatic than recessing shelves all the way round the jambs, so that they are flush to the wall.

ABOVE This actor's home in London, a converted warehouse, is spacious, but so much of the wall space is taken up with fenestration that the corridor proved the best option to store his books – that and not wanting to interfere with a minimalist aesthetic of exposed bricks and monochrome furniture.

OPPOSITE Complete with French limestone flags on the floor, the hallway at the back of this Georgian townhouse is sufficiently spacious to accommodate a modest library. The painted arch leading to the garden helps to anchor the scheme architecturally, creating, in effect, a domed block with wings.

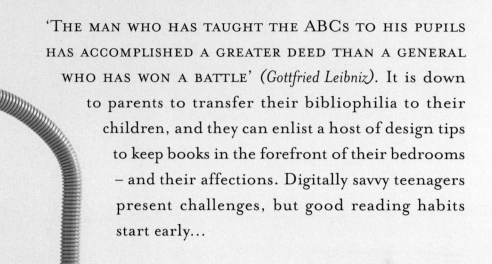

CHILDREN'S ROOMS

'THE MAN WHO HAS TAUGHT THE ABCs TO HIS PUPILS HAS ACCOMPLISHED A GREATER DEED THAN A GENERAL WHO HAS WON A BATTLE' *(Gottfried Leibniz)*. It is down to parents to transfer their bibliophilia to their children, and they can enlist a host of design tips to keep books in the forefront of their bedrooms – and their affections. Digitally savvy teenagers present challenges, but good reading habits start early...

In a child's bedroom decked out in eye-popping combinations, such as lavender, rosy-red and sky-blue, the spines of books – thin, vibrant strips; publishers' sales tools – will always fit in. The sense of order comes from the left-to-right ranking by size, and the Noah's Ark bookend, which keeps the picture books ramrod straight.

We who love books want to inculcate that love in our children. The Irish novelist John McGahern remembers becoming so wrapped up in a story when young that he didn't notice his sisters putting a straw hat on his head and untying his shoelaces; only when his chair was taken away did he 'wake out of the book'. To foster this kind of enthusiasm, books should be easily accessible and a continual backdrop to the life of a house. As Horace Mann wrote: 'A house without books is like a room without windows. No man has a right to bring up his children without surrounding them with books, if he has the means to buy them.' Since parents are their offspring's biggest influences, they should be seen with book in hand. To read to children from an early age is to solidify emotional bonds through the medium of shared narrative. As they make their first phonetic fumbles into the alphabet, we need to be patient and show that mistakes don't mean failure – they're essential to learning. We need to make connections between the characters, plots and themes of stories and the everyday dramas that make up childhood. Ultimately, we should seek to initiate a process of independent discovery that begins, in Hermann

'A HOUSE WITHOUT BOOKS IS LIKE A ROOM WITHOUT WINDOWS'

OPPOSITE Any child under two years old is liable to chew, tear or soil books if he or she gets hold of them, so a high-up perimeter shelf is a sound precaution in infancy. To guard against any accidents, the books are kept in neat piles.

BELOW Inspired by designer Shawn Soh's childhood memories of sticking letters on branches, 'A Tree Becomes a Book Becomes a Tree' changes form – flourishes and then sheds its leaves, you might say – as hooks are stacked up and removed.

LEFT Having a strong colour behind white bookshelves makes them doubly enticing for children. Antique dealer Josephine Ryan has supplied access to the upper shelves, but made reading the priority.

ABOVE This dinky set of shelves looks like it's been knocked together from a nest of old side tables. Its wheels make the whole thing easy to manoeuvre, which may or may not be a good thing depending on the children in question.

OPPOSITE These inviting chairs-cum-poufs – a designer's refinement of the bean bag – make for a companionable reading area, and can be rolled over to the window if more daylight is required.

Hesse's words, as a 'pretty garden with a tulip bed and a little fish pond; now the garden becomes a park, it becomes a landscape, a section of the earth, the world, it becomes a Paradise and the Ivory Coast, it entices with constantly new enchantments, blooms in ever-new colours'. If you ever feel despondent about the slow pace of your child's reading progress,

bear in mind that Einstein didn't learn to read until he was nine years old.

BOOK STORAGE FOR KIDS

One obvious way of keeping books at the foreground of youngsters's minds is to make sure they don't take a back seat in the interior design of their bedrooms.

PAINT THE INSIDE OF A CASE SO THAT IT CONTRASTS WITH THE OUTSIDE

Make them easily accessible and visually prominent. The spines of most picture books aimed at the under-fives are narrow – sufficiently so to require squinting in adults – so it's an excellent idea to supplement a conventional bookcase by creating a low angled lipped shelf along one wall (or two or three shorter ones above one another) on which to have a rotating display of current favourites, covers looking out. Children can get fixated on particular titles – I could recite Martin Waddell's *Owl Babies* backwards in my sleep – and since parents are the ones that have to read them aloud, they have every right to shuffle their preferences to the face-out display and return to blessed obscurity ones done to death.

Bookcases can be made eye-catching in numerous ways. Victorian houses, built before central heating was widely available, often have fireplaces with their own flues in upstairs rooms. If

ABOVE LEFT The next step after large picture books, young readers' 'chapter books' are small enough so that they can be stored in office drawers.

ABOVE RIGHT Despite the plain colours, this bedroom in Italy designed by Katrin Arens plays tricks with scale (note the three sizes of chair) that will appeal to children's rich imaginations.

OPPOSITE Combining books with toys encourages children to make reading a part of play.

encourages young children to incorporate reading – or rather, pretending to read – into play.

If siblings are sharing a bedroom, bunk beds obviously reduce the amount of floor space being taken up; you can also get models that have shelving built in. A line of books at the side of the pillow will

LEFT Books don't have to be easily to hand if they are rarely consulted things like last year's schoolbooks. And every time the little occupant of this room clambers up to get one down she will learn a little bit more about the Atlantic.

BELOW In this north London home, a salvaged wood-and-glass cabinet has been slotted strikingly into modern built-in cupboards, with a deep storage shelf above.

OPPOSITE Although this cabinet looks like it's been languishing in a field in all weathers, it's still a solid piece of joinery, apparently strong enough to take whatever little children can throw at it. The fading, flaking paintwork of the toy/book storage unit doesn't matter because the multicoloured checks of the bulletin board above (and its displays) are so vibrant.

they are in kids' bedrooms, obvious health-and-safety concerns mean that they are likely to be dead spaces. Use the small ready-made recess to build shelves for small-format books, such as the 20-title-strong 'Winnie the Pooh Classic Story Cupboard' (Egmont) or the 50-strong 'Mr Men' collection (ditto).

Children tend to love strong colours, and one can exploit this by painting the inside of a case a hue that contrasts with that of the outside. If you own a router, and are a reasonably competent carpenter, you can customize a conventional bookcase, turning it into a house (by cutting out a simple pediment) – or if it's tall and thin, a rocket (by forming a cone shape to fix to the top). Placing toys – action figures, soft animals, dolls – on the shelves alongside books

FOR TODAY'S TEENAGERS, BOOKS MUST COMPETE WITH A HOST OF OTHER MEDIA

This kind of storage unit, which combines myriad different compartments – open shelves, boxy recesses and door-fronted cupboards – encourages children to keep their room tidy by having clearly demarcated zones for different items. Its colour will ensure most grown-ups remain in the bedroom for as short a time as possible. Result!

OPPOSITE The 'Penguin Donkey 2' is a 1963 reworking by Ernest Race of the original 1939 Riss version, designed for Isokon Plus to hold Allen Lane's newly conceived paperbacks. Race's main innovation was the flat top, so that the bookcase could double as a side table. This version is made of white-painted wood with legs in cherry.

encourage reading last thing at night and first thing in the morning – and the vertical stacking of the mattresses means that lighting can be discreet and not disturb a sleeping brother or sister.

TEENAGERS' SPACES

'Perhaps it is only in childhood that books have any deep influence on our lives.' So wrote Graham Greene, who almost joined the Nigerian navy aged 19 after having read H. Rider Haggard's *King Solomon's Mines*. As the impressionable teenage years beckon, books have the potential to be hugely influential, not just in terms of career path but moulding character. As Italo Calvino put it: 'they give a form to future experiences, providing models, terms of comparison, schemes for classification, scales of value,

exemplars of beauty', and that continues to hold true long after the book read in youth has been forgotten. For today's teenagers – even those who love to read – books must compete with a host of other technologies, from computer games to mobile phones. I decry the lazy Luddite tendency among some adults who say that these digital developments will necessarily pollute young minds. The new media can be used intelligently or stupidly, and history demonstrates that all new technologies – including the invention of moveable type in the 15th century – are commonly greeted by a moral panic. Nonetheless, we should perhaps be wary of one aspect: the new media trades on sensation and immediate gratification, not states typically associated with reading. The influence of gaming and being

Judging by the central pendant and wall sconces that look like carpenter's planes, the parents of this teenager clearly have a soft spot for eccentric light fittings. A downlighter has also been wired into the fireplace, which now functions as book-storage space.

OPPOSITE LEFT More crafty wiring is apparent in this recess in a teenager's bedroom, custom-designed to gain maximum cool points from his friends. What is essentially a bedside table has been built into the alcove formed by a chimneybreast. Downlighters illuminate the books and make reading in the legless platform bed possible.

OPPOSITE RIGHT Books offer surprisingly effective sound insulation, a point well worth considering as your teenager ramps up the volume when you're out. Neighbours may well benefit from the tactful placement of speakers.

able to invent an online identity partly explains why paranormal romance and sci-fi and fantasy are such popular genres among teenagers. All the advice points to encouraging them to read whatever they want, so long as they are reading; but one should always make the grown-ups' books readily available. After all, this is how most children progress to a mature literary life.

Since teenagers need to study, it is a good idea to have a separate shelf above a desk area where textbooks can be combined with reference books. Help them to form a capsule library, including a concise atlas, a picture-heavy zoology book and

an art history, as well as an illustrated encyclopedia and single-volume dictionary. A loft bed with a ladder offers privacy, and also frees up space for shelves beneath; some manufacturers offer the reverse arrangement, with a storage zone placed on top of a bed. Since teenagers often like to alter their set-up it's a good idea to have furnishings that are adaptable, even makeshift. A bean bag makes for a comfortable reading area that can be easily shifted to a window during daylight and next to a lamp when it's dark. Likewise, a crate can easily be turned into a bookcase – and because it's so cheap, it doesn't matter if it's customized in an outlandish

An open-plan study space for two teenagers stands across from a bedroom for one of them that can be partitioned with the help of pocket doors. The Artemide reading light, plus the matching laptops and designer chairs, suggests an adult's office until one spies the lava lamp, the tennis trophies and the propped-up bass guitar.

way. The old student standby of planks and bricks is surprisingly visually effective; it is also very portable and the height of shelves readily adjustable. Furthermore, it's an instant no-skills-required DIY solution in which your child can take charge of his or her own space. One can also buy folding bookcases that can be swiftly flatpacked – ideal for the son or daughter who will be moving digs every year at university or college.

ALL NEW TECHNOLOGIES – INCLUDING
THE INVENTION OF MOVEABLE TYPE – ARE
COMMONLY GREETED BY A MORAL PANIC

SELECT BIBLIOGRAPHY

Julian Barnes
The Pedant in the Kitchen
(Atlantic, 2004)

Nicholas A. Basbanes
A Gentle Madness: Bibliophiles, Bibliomanes and the Eternal Passion for Books
(St Martin's Press, 1999)

Estelle Ellis and Caroline Seebohm
At Home with Books: How Booklovers Live with and Care for Their Libraries
(Thames & Hudson, 2006)

Anne Fadiman
Ex Libris: Confessions of a Common Reader
(Farrar, Straus & Giroux, 2000)

Leslie Geddes-Brown
Books Do Furnish a Room
(Merrell, 2009)

Steven Gilbar (ed.)
Reading in Bed: Personal Essays on the Glories of Reading
(David R. Godine, 1998)

Holbrook Jackson
Bookman's Pleasure: A Recreation for Book Lovers
(Farrar, Straus & Co, 1947)

Rob Kaplan and
Harold Rabinowitz (eds)
A Passion for Books: A Book Lover's Treasury
(Times Books, 2001)

Rob Kaplan and
Harold Rabinowitz (eds)
Speaking of Books: The Best Things Ever Said about Books and Book Collecting
(Crown, 2001)

Alberto Manguel
A History of Reading
(Flamingo, 1997)

Henry Petroski
The Book on the Bookshelf
(Vintage, 2000)

Alan Powers
Living with Books
(Mitchell Beazley, 2006)

Francis Spufford
The Child that Books Built
(Faber & Faber, 2002)

Linda Wolfe
The Literary Gourmet: Menus from Masterpieces
(Random House, 1962)

RESOURCES and SUPPLIERS

WEBSITES

www.abebooks.com
An online book marketplace connecting readers to thousands of booksellers offering new, second-hand, rare and out-of-print titles.

www.biguniverse.com
Award-winning US-based web community aimed at young readers, in which they can read online, recommend books, and create and publish their own works.

www.bookcoverarchive.com
Thousands of book covers 'for the purpose of appreciation and categorisation'. But can you judge the contents by them?

www.bookmooch.com
Free online service enabling readers to give away books they no longer want and get books in return.

bookshelfporn.com
...For hardcore bibliophiles to feast their eyes on.

www.guardian.co.uk/childrens-books-site
Excellent site where children can write reviews and discuss books with their peers.

www.gutenberg.org
Project Gutenberg was the first site to offer free ebooks online. More than 30,000 titles available.

theblogonthebookshelf.blogspot.com
Wonderful and wacky bookshelves – soon to be made into a book by Thames & Hudson.

www.wordpool.co.uk
Children's book site for parents, teachers and writers.

BOOKCASE and SHELVING SUPPLIERS

UK

Lombok
Handmade bookcases in mostly dark woods.
+44 (0)870 240 7380
www.lombok.co.uk

Shelfstore
Flexible modular self-assembly pine bookshelves, offered in a variety of heights, depths and widths.
+44 (0)1628 782642
www.shelvingsystem.co.uk

Skandium
A wide range of modern shelving by Scandinavian designers.
+44 (0)20 7584 2066
www.skandium.com

Unto This Last
Unusual birch-ply shelving made with innovative digital tools.
230 Brick Lane, London E2 7EB
+44 (0)20 7613 0882
www.untothislast.co.uk

US

Book Hut
Agent for Hale Manufacturing, one of America's leading institutional suppliers of hardwood bookcases.
+1 702 285 4437
www.thebookcasepeople.com

Moss
High-end European-flavoured
modern design in New York.
150 Greene Street,
New York, NY 10012
+1 212 204 7100
www.mossonline.com

GREAT BOOKSHOPS

UK

Barter Books
Set in an old Victorian railway
station, this used and exchange
bookshop was described by *New
Statesman* as 'the British Library
of second-hand books'.
Alnwick Station, Alnwick,
Northumberland NE66 2NP
+44 (0)1665 604888
www.barterbooks.co.uk

Bernard J. Shapero Rare Books
One of London's leading
antiquarian bookshops.
32 Saint George Street
London W1S 2EA
+44 (0)20 7493 0876
www.shapero.com

Daunt Books
An original Edwardian bookshop
with long oak galleries and
graceful skylights.
83 Marylebone High Street
London W1U 4QW
+44 (0)20 7224 2295
www.dauntbooks.co.uk

Hatchards
Trading since 1797, this is the
most aristocratic of bookshops,
with three royal warrants.
187 Piccadilly, London W1J 9LE
+44 (0)20 7439 9921
www.hatchards.co.uk

US

City Lights
A bastion of alternative culture
and the West Coast's literary
hotspot since the 1950s.
261 Columbus Avenue,
San Francisco, CA 94133
+1 415 362 8193
www.citylights.com

Printed Matter
Art books of all stripes.
195 Tenth Avenue
New York, NY 10011
+1 212 925 0325
www.printedmatter.org

St Mark's Bookshop
Unequalled devotion to classic
and cutting-edge books.
31 Third Avenue
New York, NY 10003
+1 212 260 7853
www.stmarksbookshop.com

ORGANISATIONS AND LITERARY FESTIVALS

UK

Booktrust
Independent UK-wide charity
dedicated to helping people of all
ages and cultures to enjoy books.
+44 (0)20 8516 2977
www.booktrust.org.uk

The Poetry Society
Its mission is to advance the
study, use and enjoyment of
poetry.
+44 (0)20 7420 9880
www.poetrysociety.org.uk

The Telegraph Hay Festival
One of the world's biggest –
'the Woodstock of the mind'
(Bill Clinton)
+44 (0)1497 822629
www.hayfestival.com

**Times Cheltenham Literature
Festival**
One of the oldest and best loved
in the world.
+44 (0)1242 505444
www.cheltenhamfestivals.com

US

The Center for Book Arts
Committed to cultivating
the book as an art object.
28 West 27th Street
New York, NY 10001
+1 212 481 0295
www.centerforbookarts.org

**The Fellowship of American
Bibliophilic Societies**
A federation of book-loving
organisations.
www.fabsbooks.org

National Book Festival
Held in Washington DC in early
autumn, it attracts tens of
thousands of people annually.
Organised by the Library of
Congress.
+1 202 707 5000
www.loc.gov/bookfest

Talas
Serving professionals and
amateurs with hand bookbinding
and conservation supplies.
330 Morgan Avenue, Brooklyn,
New York, NY 11211
+1 212 219 0770
www.talasonline.com

Wordstock
Annual two-day literary festival
held in Portland, Oregon – one
of the largest in the US.
+1 503 549 7887
www.wordstockfestival.com

INTERNATIONAL

Fine Press Book Association
Transatlantic organisation
interested in the art of fine
printing.
www.fpba.com

**PEN World Voices: The New York
Festival of International Literature**
This year more than 100 writers
from 40 nations took part.
www.pen.org

BEAUTIFUL LIBRARIES
ROUND THE WORLD

Abbey Library
Saint Gallen, Switzerland
www.stiftsbibliothek.ch

Bodleian Library
Oxford, United Kingdom
www.bodleian.ox.ac.uk

Boston Athenaeum
Boston, Massachusetts, USA
www.bostonathenaeum.org

George Peabody Library,
Baltimore, Maryland, USA
www.library.jhu.edu

Library of Congress
Washington DC, USA
www.loc.gov

National Library of Austria
Vienna, Austria
www.onb.ac.at

New York Public Library
New York, USA
www.nypl.org

Reading Room, British Museum
London, United Kingdom
www.britishmuseum.org

Real Gabinete Português de Leitura
Rio de Janeiro, Brazil
www.realgabinete.com.br

**Strahov Monastery, Theological
Library**
Prague, Czech Republic
www.strahovskyklaster.cz/library

Trinity College Library
(The Long Room), Dublin, Ireland
www.tcd.ie/library

Wiblingen Monastery Library,
Ulm, Germany
www.kloster-wiblingen.de/en

PICTURE CREDITS

KEY: *ph*= photographer, **a**=above, **b**=below, **r**=right, **l**=left, **c**=centre.

Page **1** *ph* Polly Wreford/the home of stylist Twig Hutchinson in London; **2** *ph* Polly Wreford/the Sussex home of Paula Barnes of www.elizabarnes.com; **3l** © CICO Books ph Simon Brown/Tullynally, Ireland; **3c** ph Chris Tubbs/Ben Pentreath's London flat; **3r** © CICO Books *ph* Simon Brown/Mount Rivers; **4–5** image of Paperback shelves courtesy of Studio Parade; **6** *ph* Chris Everard/Simon and Coline Gillespie's home in North London, **7a** Baron von Humboldt (1769–1859) in his library (colour litho)/After Eduard Hilderbrandt/The Bridgeman Art Library/Getty Images; **7bl** © CICO Books *ph* Simon Brown/Stradbally Hall, Ireland; **8** *ph* Polly Wreford/London house by Sarah Delaney Design; **9l** *ph* Winfried Heinze/Trine and William Miller's home in London; **9r** *ph* Chris Everard/Adèle Lakhdari's home in Milan designed by Tito Canella of Canella & Achilli Architects; **10** *ph* Andrew Wood/Nanna Ditzel; **11** *ph* Debi Treloar/Sigolène Prébois of Tsé &Tsé associeés home in Paris; **12–13** *ph* Polly Wreford/the house of stylist and designer Ulrika Lundgren of Rika; **14** *ph* Debi Treloar/the home of Kristin Norris and Trevor Lunn, Philadelphia; **15l** *ph* Chris Everard/Yuen-Wei Chew's apartment in London designed by Paul Daly Design Studio Ltd; **15ar** *ph* Winfried Heinze/the Notting Hill flat of Ebba Thott from "Sigmar" in London; **15br & 16al** *ph* Dan Duchars; **16ar** *ph* Catherine Gratwicke; **16b** *ph* Andrew Woods/Paul & Carolyn Morgan, Wales; **17** *ph* Catherine Gratwicke/architect François Muracciole's apartment in Paris; **18** *ph* Polly Wreford/the home in Copenhagen of designer Birgitte Raben Olrik of Raben Saloner; **19l** *ph* Polly Wreford/the family home of the stylist Anja Koops and chef Alain Parry in Amsterdam; **19ar** *ph* Debi Treloar; **19br** *ph* Polly Wreford/Robert Levithan Residence, New York City; **20al** *ph* Debi Treloar/the London home of Rebecca Hill of *French Country Living*; **20ar** *ph* Debi Treloar; **20b** *ph* Claire Richardson/Marianne Cotterill's house in London; **21a** *ph* Debi Treloar/Annelie Bruijn's home in Amsterdam; **21b** both *ph* Debi Treloar/a London apartment designed by James Soane and Christopher Ash of Project Orange; **22l** *ph* Polly Wreford/the home of stylist Twig Hutchinson in London; **22r & 23** *ph* Jan Baldwin/Jo Berryman's home in London; **24–25** *ph* Debi Treloar/the home of Kristin Norris and Trevor Lunn, Philadelphia; **26–27 main** © Vitsoe; **27r** *ph* Alan Williams/Margot Feldman's house in New York designed by Patricia Seidman of Mullman Seidman Architects; **28l** *ph* Polly Wreford/Francesca Mills; **28r** *ph* Winfried Heinze/Florence & John Pearse's apartment in London; **29l** *ph* Jan Baldwin/carpentry & joinery by Martin Brown, painting by Taylors Interiors Ltd; **29r** Nook Coffee Table © David Pickett; **30** *ph* Jan Baldwin/Philip & Lisskulla Wagner's cottage in Sussex designed by Philip Wagner Architects; **31a** *ph* Polly Wreford/the Sussex home of Paula Barnes of www.elizabarnes.com; **31b** © CICO Books *ph* Mark Scott; **32** *ph* Chris Everard/Ruth Artmonsky's loft in Covent Garden; **33** *ph* Debi Treloar/the house of Assaï in Paris; **34l** *ph* Catherine Gratwicke; **34r & 35** *ph* Polly Wreford/Marina Coriasco; **36** *ph* Andrew Wood/the home of Ellen Weiman & Dubi Silverstein in New York, designed by architects Ogawa/Depardon; **37l** *ph* Chris Everard/Tim & Celia Holman's house in London, designed by DIVE Architects Ltd; **37ar** *ph* Chris Everard/Manhattan home of designer Matthew Patrick Smyth; **37br** *ph* Jan Baldwin/Mona Nerenberg & Lisa Bynon, Sag Harbor; **38** *ph* Jan Baldwin/Cressida Granger of Mathmos' cottage in Dorset; **39** Bibliochaise by .nobody&co. srl © .nobody&co. srl; **40al** *ph* Catherine Gratwicke/gallery and bookshop owner, Françoise de Nobele's apartment in Paris; **40ac & b** *ph* Catherine Gratwicke/Kari Sigerson's apartment in New York; **40ar** *ph* Andrew Wood/Urban Salon Architects; **41** *ph* Andrew Wood/Jane Collins of Sixty 6 in Marylebone High Street, London; **42** © Vitsoe; **43** *ph* Polly Wreford/Alex White; **44** *ph* Claire Richardson/the home of Fiona and Woody Woodhouse in Herefordshire; **45** *ph* Jan Baldwin/Alfredo Paredes and Brad Goldfarb's loft in Tribeca, New York designed by Michael Neumann Architecture; **46a** image of T-shelf courtesy of and designed by J1 studio; **46b** image courtesy of Contraforma – Shelf Quad in walnut brown by Nauris Kalinauskas; **46–47** *ph* Paul Ryan/the home of Nils Tunebjer in Sweden; **48** both *ph* Chris Everard/Simon Crookall's apartment in London designed by Urban Salon; **49a** *ph* Debi Treloar/the restaurant "Derriere" designed and owned by the "Hazouz Brothers"; **49bl** Blockshelf © Amy Hunting; **49br** *ph* Winfried Heinze/a Parisian pied-a-terre designed by Marianne Pascal for an Anglo-French couple; **50** *ph* Debi Treloar/Katrin Arens; **51** *ph* Debi Treloar/the London home of Richard Moore; **52–53** *ph* Jan Baldwin/Chris Dyson Architects; **54** *ph* Simon Brown © CICO Books/Castle Dodard; **55** *ph* Claire Richardson/the home of Jean-Louis Fages and Matthieu Ober in Nimes; **56–57** © CICO Books *ph* Simon Brown/Tullynally, Ireland; **58** *ph* Lisa Cohen/the home in London of Abigail Ahern, www.atelierabigailahern.com; **59** *ph* Chris Everard/an apartment in Milan designed by Nicoletta Marazza; **60** *ph* Claire Richardson/Gérard and Danièlle Labre's home near Uzès in France; **61** *ph* Chris Everard/David Mullman's apartment in New York designed by Mullman Seidman Architects; **62** © CICO Books *ph* Simon Brown/Tullynally, Ireland; **63** *ph* Chris Tubbs/Powers house, London; **64** library staircase by Levitate Architect & Design Studio & Rodrigues Associates, Structural Engineers, image courtesy of Levitate; **65al** *ph* Chris Everard/designer Helen Ellery, London; **65ar** *ph* Debi Treloar/the London home of Tracey Boyd and Adrian Wright; **65b** *ph* Catherine Gratwicke; **66** *ph* Jan Baldwin/Jo Berryman's home in London; **67** *ph* Alan Williams/New York apartment designed by Bruce Bierman; **68** *ph* Winfried Heinze/the apartment of Yancey and Mark Richardson in New York, architecture and interior design by Steven Learner Studio. Nudes on desk by

Alvin Booth; **69 *ph*** Andrew Wood/the home of Ellen Weiman & Dubi Silverstein in New York, designed by architects Ogawa/Depardon; **70 *ph*** Chris Tubbs/Teresa Ginori's home near Varese-parchment lampshade by architect Roberto Gerosa; **71 *ph*** Chris Everard/John Nicolson's house in Spitalfields, London; **72 *ph*** Polly Wreford/designer Lisette Pleasance and Mick Shaw's home and B&B; **73 *ph*** Polly Wreford/the home in Provençe of Carolyn Oswald; **74–75** image courtesy of Alternative Plans-Modulnova's 'My Kitchen' collection in a white gloss polymeric finish and black matt wave polymeric finish from Alternative Plans; **76 *ph*** Chris Everard/Tim & Celia Holman's house in London, designed by DIVE Architects Ltd; **77 *ph*** Lisa Cohen/the home in London of Abigail Ahern, www.atelierabigailahern.com; **78** image courtesy of Alternative Plans- Modulnova's 'Twenty' and 'My Kitchen' kitchen collections available from Alternative Plans; **79 *ph*** Winfried Heinze/interior stylist Sidsel Zachariassen; **80 *ph*** Debi Treloar/the home of Kristin Norris and Trevor Lunn, Philadelphia; **81l *ph*** Polly Wreford/the family home of the stylist Anja Koops and chef Alain Parry in Amsterdam; **81r** image courtesy of Contraforma – Quad shelf by Nauris Kalinauskas; **82 *ph*** Polly Wreford/the home in Denmark of Charlotte Gueniau of RICE; **83al *ph*** Polly Wreford/Foster House at www.beachstudios.co.uk; **83ar *ph*** Polly Wreford/Paul & Claire's beach house, East Sussex, design by www.davecoote.com, location to hire through www.beachstudios.co.uk; **83bl *ph*** Debi Treloar/the London home of Sam Robinson, co-owner of 'The Cross' and 'Cross the Road; **84l *ph*** Chris Everard/John Nicolson's house in Spitalfields, London; **84–85c *ph*** Chris Tubbs/Powers house, London; **85r *ph*** Polly Wreford/the family home of Sarah and Mark Benton in Rye; **86a *ph*** Chris Everard/Lisa & Richard Frisch's apartment in New York designed by Patricia Seidman of Mullman Seidman Architects, interior decoration by Mariette Himes Gomez; **86b *ph*** Debi Treloar/John Derian's apartment in New York; **87 *ph*** Paul Massey/all items from Cote Jardin boutique; **88 *ph*** Chris Tubbs/Simon and Antonia Johnson's home in Somerset; **89 *ph*** Claire Richardson/the home of Spencer and Freya Swaffer in Arundel; **90 & 91 *ph*** Chris Everard/Yuen-Wei Chew's apartment in London designed by Paul Daly Design Studio Ltd; **92–93** both ***ph*** Andrew Wood/an original Florida home restored by Andrew Weaving of Century, www.centuryd.com; **94 *ph*** Chris Everard/Gentucca Bini's apartment in Milan; **95l *ph*** Andrew Wood/Paul & Carolyn Morgan's house in Wales; **95ar *ph*** Polly Wreford/the family home of the stylist Anja Koops and chef Alain Parry in Amsterdam; **95br *ph*** Debi Treloar/design Cecilia Proserpio, furniture Katrin Arens; **96 & 97 *ph*** Debi Treloar/the home and studio of the art & craft artist Nathalie Lete in Paris; **98 *ph*** Polly Wreford/home of 27.12 Design Ltd., Chelsea, NYC; **99 *ph*** Debi Treloar/family home, Bankside, London-DIVE Architects; **100l *ph*** Jan Baldwin/Chris Dyson Architects; **100–101 *ph*** Debi Treloar/Marcus Hewitt and Susan Hopper's home in Litchfield County, Connecticut; **102–103 *ph*** Debi Treloar/the family home of Nina Tolstrup and Jack Mama of www.studiomama.com; **104** © CICO Books ***ph*** Simon Brown/Higginsbrook; **105l *ph*** Jan Baldwin/Jane Moran's cottage in Sussex; **105r** © CICO Books ***ph*** Simon Brown/Castle Dodard; **106 *ph*** Jan Baldwin/designer Helen Ellery's home in London; **107 *ph*** Polly Wreford/Paul & Claire's beach house, East Sussex – design www.davecoote.com, location to hire through www.beachstudios.co.uk; **108al *ph*** Alan Williams/Margot Feldman's house in New York designed by Patricia Seidman of Mullman Seidman Architects; **108bl *ph*** Dan Duchars; **108br *ph*** Chris Everard/Sig.ra Venturini's apartment in Milan; **108ar & 109** both ***ph*** Dan Duchars; **110 *ph*** Polly Wreford/Foster House at www.beachstudios.co.uk; **111** © CICO Books ***ph*** Mark Scott; **112 *ph*** Polly Wreford/Robert Levithan Residence, New York City; **113 *ph*** Polly Wreford/Glenn Carwithen & Sue Miller's house in London; **114l *ph*** Polly Wreford/a family home in London designed by Marion Lichtig; **114r *ph*** Chris Everard; **115 *ph*** Debi Treloar/Robert Elms and Christina Wilson's family home in London; **116–117** both ***ph*** Christopher Drake/Andrea Spencer's house in London; **118 *ph*** Jan Baldwin/Jane Moran's cottage in Sussex; **119** © CICO Books ***ph*** Simon Brown/Ballytrasna; **120l *ph*** Catherine Gratwicke; **120r & 121** library staircase by Levitate Architect & Design Studio & Rodrigues Associates, Structural Engineers, image courtesy of Levitate; **122 *ph*** Polly Wreford/home of architect Reinhard Weiss & Bele Weiss in London; **123 *ph*** Polly Wreford/Foster House at www.beachstudios.co.uk; **124 *ph*** Jan Baldwin/designer Helen Ellery's home in London; **125 *ph*** Polly Wreford/Robert Levithan Residence, New York City; **126–127 *ph*** Chris Tubbs/Giorgio & Ilaria Miani's Podere Buon Riposo in Val d'Orcia (available to rent); **127r *ph*** Chris Everard/an apartment in Milan designed by Nicoletta Marazza; **128 *ph*** Polly Wreford/Paul & Claire's beach house, East Sussex, design by www.davecoote.com, location to hire through www.beachstudios.co.uk; **129 *ph*** Winfried Heinze; **130 *ph*** Chris Everard/an actor's London home designed by Site Specific; **131 *ph*** Christopher Drake/Dick & Vanessa Cooper's house in London designed by Eger Architects; **132–133 *ph*** Chris Everard/Tim & Celia Holman's house in London, designed by DIVE Architects Ltd; **134** ph Winfried Heinze/Josephine Ryan's house in London; **135** 'A tree becomes a book becomes a tree' © Shawn Soh; **136l *ph*** Winfried Heinze/Josephine Ryan's house in London; **136l *ph*** Winfried Heinze/a family home in Brighton; **137 *ph*** Winfried Heinze/family house designed by Henri Fitzwilliam-Lay; **138l *ph*** Winfried Heinze; **138r *ph*** Debi Treloar/Katrin Arens; **139 *ph*** Debi Treloar/Sudi Pigott's house in London; **140l *ph*** Polly Wreford/the family home of Elisabeth and Scott Wotherspoon, owners of Wickle in Lewes, www.wickle.co.uk; **140r *ph*** Winfried Heinze/a family home in North London designed by Sally Mackereth of Wells Mackereth Architects; **141 *ph*** Debi Treloar/Victoria Andreae's house in London; **142–143** main ***ph*** Debi Treloar/new build house in Notting Hill designed by Seth Stein Architects; **143r *ph*** Debi Treloar; **144 & 145l *ph*** Winfried Heinze/Madame Sera Hersham-Loftus's home; **145r *ph*** Winfried Heinze/the home of Ben Johns and Deb Waterman Johns; **146–147 *ph*** Winfried Heinze/Dr Alex Sherman and Ms Ivy Baer Sherman's residence in New York City – Mullman Seidman Architects.

ARCHITECTS, ARTISTS, DESIGNERS and BUSINESS OWNERS

WHOSE WORK HAS BEEN FEATURED IN THIS BOOK

27.12 Design Ltd
333 Hudson Street
10th Floor
New York, NY 10014
+1 212 727 8169
www.2712design.com
Page 98

Alternative Plans
4 Hester Road
London SW11 4AN
+44 (0)20 3375 2468
www.alternative-plans.co.uk
Pages 74–75, 78

Amy Hunting
+44 (0)7501 821218
www.amyhunting.com
hello@amyhunting.com
Page 49bl

Anja Koops
fashion & interior styling:
Anjakoops@hetnet.nl
and
Alain Parry's restaurant:
www.balthazarskeuken.nl
Pages 19l, 81l, 95ar

Annelie Brun
+31 653 702869
Annelie_bruijn@email.com
Page 21a

Anthropologie
www.anthropologie.com
Pages 14, 24–25, 80

Atelier Abigail Ahern
137 Upper Street
Islington
London N1 1QP
+44 (0)20 7354 8181
www.atelierabigailahern.com
contact@atelierbypost.com
Pages 58, 77

Atlanta Bartlett
www.atlantabartlett.com
Pages 83al, 83ar, 107, 110, 123, 128

Beach Studios
www.beachstudios.co.uk
Pages 83al, 83ar, 107, 110, 123, 128

Ben Johns CEO
Scout Ltd
(bags and floor coverings)
1055 Thomas Jefferson Street NW
Washington DC 20007
+1 202 944 9590
ben@bungalowco.com
Page 145r

Ben Pentreath Ltd
17 Rugby Street
Bloomsbury
London WC1N 3QT
+44 (0)20 7430 2526
www.benpentreath.com
info@benpentreath.com
Page 3c

Bexon Woodhouse Creative
www.bexonwoodhouse.com
Page 44

Birgitte Raben Olrik
www.rabenssaloner.com
Page 18

Bloom
43 Madison Street
Sag Harbor, NY 11963
+1 631 725 5940
Page 37br

Bruce Bierman Design Inc
29 West 15th Street
New York, NY 10011
+1 212 243 1935
www.biermandesign.com
info@biermandesign.com
Page 67

Canella & Achilli Architetti
Via Revere 9
20123 Milano
Italy
+39 0 24 69 52 22
www.canella-achilli.com
info@canella-achilli.com
Page 9r

Cecile Daladier artist and Nicolas Soulier
architect
assai@free.fr
Page 33

Cecilia Proserpio
cecilia.proserpio@fastwebnet
.it
Page 95br

Century Design
68 Marylebone High Street
London W1M 3AQ
www.centuryd.com
modern@centuryd.com
Pages 92–93 both

Chris Dyson Architects
11 Princelet Street
Spitalfields
London E1 6QH
Pages 52–53, 100l

Christina Wilson
www.christinawilson.co.uk
Page 115

CONTRAFORMA
Shelf Quad by Nauris Kalinauskas
Contra Design House
Shevcenkos str 16A,
Vilnius 03111
Lithuania
+37 0 690 17000
www.contraforma.com
Page 81r

Cote Jardin
Place du Marche
17590 Ars En Re
France
Page 87

Dave Coote Design
www.davecootedesign.com
Pages 83ar, 107, 128

David Pickett
+1 440 420 9074
www.david-pickett.com
dpickett@student.cia.edu
Page 29r

Deb Waterman Johns
Get Dressed Wardrobe and Home & Fifi
1633 29th Street NW
Washington DC 20007
+1 202 625 6425
deb@dogbunny.com
Page 145r

Derriere
69 rue des Gravilliers
75003 Paris
France
+33 (0)1 44 61 91 95
Page 49a

DIVE Architects AB
Gästrikegatan 20
S-113 62 Stockholm
Sweden
+46 8 33 10 30
www.divearchitects.com
mail@divearchitects.com
*Pages 37l, 76, 99,
132–133*

Eger Architects
Architects & Landscape
Architects
2 D'Eynsford Road
London SE5 7EB
+44 (0)20 7701 6771
www.egerarchitects.com
design@egerarchitects.com
Page 131

**Eliza Barnes
Architectural Salvage
and Design**
+44 (0)7977 234896
www.elizabarnes.com
Pages 2, 31a

Francesca Mills
www.francescamills.com
Page 28l

François Muracciole
Architect
francois@fmuracciole.com
www.fmuracciole.com
Page 17

French Country Living
f.c.l.com@wanadoo.fr
+44 (0)7770 520371
www.frenchcountryliving
 antiques.com
Page 20al

Galerie de Nobele
2 rue de Bourbon le
Château
75006 Paris
France
Page 40al

**Gérard and Danièlle
Labre**
2 boulevard Alliés
30700 Uzès
France
+33 (0)6 20 69 70 32
glabre@orange.fr
Page 60

Helen Ellery
I Love Home
Interiors and stylist
helen@helenellery.com
helene@i-love-home.co.uk
Pages 65al, 106, 124

**Henri Fitzwilliam-Lay
Ltd**
+44 (0)7968 948053
hfitz@hotmail.com
Page 137

Ilaria Miani
Shop
Via Monserrato 35
00186 Roma
Italy
+39 0668 33160
www.ilariamiani.it
ilariamiani@tin.it
Pages 126–127

J1studio
Jaewon Cho
www.j1studio.com
info@j1studio.com

Jean-Louis Fages
Antiquites – Décoration
(Nimes) Sarl Interieur
Ganache
3 Place du Marché
30000 Nimes
France
+33 (0)4 66 27 38 23
matao11@hotmail.fr
Page 55

Jo Berryman
Interior/events design
and styling
www.matrushka.co.uk
Pages 22r, 23, 66

John Derian
Store
6 East 2nd Street
New York, NY 10003
+1 212 677 3917
www.johnderian.com
Page 86b

John Nicolson
House available to hire
as a location at:
johnnynicolson@aol.com
Pages 71, 84l

John Pearse, Tailor
6 Meard Street
London W1F OEG
+44 (0)20 7434 0738
jp@johnpearse .co.uk
www.johnpearse.co.uk
Page 28r

Josephine Ryan
www.josephineryanantiques.
 co.uk
Pages 134, 136l

Judd Street Gallery
www.juddstreetgallery.com
Pages 63, 84–85c

Katrin Arens
www.katrinarens.it
info@katrinarens.it
Pages 50, 95br, 138r

**Kristin Norris and Trevor
Lunn**
Managing Director of
BHLDN
www.BHLDN.com
Executive Creative
Director of
Anthropologie
www.anthroplogie.com
Pages 14, 24–25, 80

L E V I T A T E
Architecture and design
studio limited
161 Roseberry Avenue
London EC1R 4QX
+44 (0)20 7833 4455
www.levitate.uk.com
studio@levitate.uk.com
Pages 64, 120r, 121

Lisette Pleasance
Boonshill Farm B&B
Nr Rye
East Sussex TN31 7QA
www.boonshillfarm.co.uk
Page 72

Marianne Cotterill
www.mariannecotterill.com
Page 20b

**Marianne Pascal
Architecte D.P.L.G.**
85 rue Albert
75013 Paris
France
+33 (0)1 45 86 60 01
www.mariannepascal.com
Page 49br

Mariette Himes Gomez
www.gomezassociates.com
Page 86a

Marion Lichtig
+44 (0)20 8458 6658
www.marionlichtig.co.uk
marionlichtig@hotmail.
 co.uk
Page 114l

Martin Brown
+44 (0)20 7834 6747
Page 29l

Mathmos
+44 (0)20 7549 2700
www.mathmos.com
Page 38

Matthew Patrick Smyth Inc.
136 East 57th Street
Suite 1700
New York, NY 10022
+1 212 333 5353
www.matthewsmyth.com
Page 37ar

Michael Neumann Architecture
11 East 88th Street
New York, NY 10128
+ 1 212 828 0407
www.mnarch.com
Page 45

Mullman Seidman Architects
137 Varick Street
New York, NY 10013
+1 212 431 0770
www.mullmanseidman.com
Pages 27r, 61, 86a, 108al, 146–147

Nanna Ditzel Design A/S
www.nanna-ditzel-design.dk
Page 10

Nathalie Lete
www.nathalie-lete.com
Pages 96, 97

Nicoletta Marazza
Via G. Morone, 8
20121 Milan
Italy
+39 2 7601 4482
Pages 59, 127r

Nina Tolstrup
STUDIOMAMA
www.studiomama.com
Pages 102–103

.nobody&co. srl
via Camperio, 9
20123 Milan
Italy
www.nobodyandco.com
Page 39

NONAH! mobilier
par nature
www.nonah.fr
bonjour@nonah.fr
+33 (0)9 70 44 07 80

Ogawa/Depardon Architects
Architect: Gilles Depardon
69 Mercer Street
2nd Floor
New York, NY 10012
+1 212 627 7390
www.oda-ny.com
info@oda-ny.com
Pages 36, 69

Paul Daly Design Studio Ltd
11 Hoxton Square
London N1 6NU
+44 (0)20 7613 4855
www.pauldaly.com
studio@pauldaly.com
Pages 15l, 90, 91

Philip Wagner Architects
Architecture Planning
Interior Design
5 Ladbroke Road
London W11 3PA
+44 (0)20 7221 3219
www.philipwagner.co.uk
mailbox@philipwagner.co.uk
Page 30

Project Orange
+44 (0)20 7566 0410
www.projectorange.com
Page 21b both

Reinhard Weiss
3s Architects LLP
47 High Street
Kingston upon Thames
Surry KT1 1LQ
+44 (0)20 8549 2000
www.3sarchitects.com
reinhard.weiss@3sarchitects.com
Page 122

RLdesign
+1 212 741 9762
www.robertlevithan.com
rlevithan@earthlink.net
Pages 19br, 112, 125

RICE
www.rice.dk
Page 82

Richard Moore
Creative Consultant to
the Retail Industry
Scenographic
+44 (0)7958 740045
www.scenographic,blogspot.com
Page 51

ROLLO Contemporary Art
17 Compton Terrace
London N1 2UN
+44 (0)20 7493 8383
www.rolloart.com
Page 6

Sarah Benton
Lion Street Store
A Design led Family Store
No.6 Lion Street
Rye
East Sussex TN31 7NB
+44 (0)7921 709217
www.lionstreetstore.co.uk
Page 85r

Sarah Delaney Design
+44 (0)20 7221 2010
www.sarahdelaneydesign.co.uk
info@sarahdelaneydesign.co.uk
Page 8

Sera Hersham-Loftus
www.seraoflondon.com
Pages 144, 145l

Seth Stein Architects
15 Grand Union Centre
West Row
Ladbroke Grove
London W10 5AS
+44 (0)20 8968 8581
www.sethstein.com
Pages 142–143 main

Shawn Soh
www.designartist.co.kr
shawnsoh@naver.com
Page 135

Sidsel Zachariassen
Stenderupgade 1 1tv
1738 Copenhagen V
Denmark
www.sidselz.dk
Page 79

Sigmar
263 Kings Road
London SW3 5EL
+44 (0)20 7751 5802
www.sigmarlondon.com
Page 15ar

Silence
Creative research design
consultancy
+44 (0)1273 299231
www.silence.co.uk
Page 136l

Site Specific Ltd
305 Curtain House
134–146 Curtain Road
London EC2A 3AR
+44 (0)20 7689 3200
www.sitespecificltd.co.uk
office@sitespecificltd.co.uk
Page 130

Sixty 6
66 Marylebone High
Street, Marylebone
London W1U 5JF
+44 (0)20 7224 6066
Page 41

**Spencer Swaffer
Antiques**
30 High Street
Arundel
West Sussex BN18 9AB
+44 (0)1903 882132
www.spencerswaffer.com
Page 89

Steven Learner Studio
307 7th Avenue
Room 2201
New York, NY 10001
www.stevenlearnerstudio.
  com/index.htm
mstevens@stevenlearnerstu
  dio.com
Page 68

**Studio Parade Paulien
Berendsen en Eric Sloot**
L. van Veghelstraat 25
5212 AD 's-
Hertogenbosch
Netherlands
+31 (0)73 6123707
www.studioparade.nl
contact@studioparade.nl
Pages 4–5

Studio Roderick Vos
Postbus 31
5256 ZG
Heusden Vesting
Netherlands
+31 (0)416 666222
www.roderickvosshop.nl
info@roderickvos.com
Pages 4–5

Taylors Interiors Ltd
+44 (0)20 7730 3000
Page 29l

Teresa Ginori
Teresa.ginori@aliceposta.it
Page 70

**The Cross and
Cross the Road**
141 Portland Road
London W11 4LR
+44 (0)20 7727 6760
Page 83bl

Tracey Boyd
www.traceyboyd.com
Page 65ar

Tsé &Tsé associeés
Catherine Lévy &
Sigolène Prébois
www.tse-tse.com
Page 11

Twig Hutchison
www.twighutchison.com
Pages 1, 22l

Ulrika Lundgren
Rikaint B.V.
Oude Spiegelstraat 9
1016 BM Amsterdam
Netherlands
+31 20 33 01112
www.rikaint.com
rika_sales@mac.com
Pages 12–13

Urban Salon Ltd
Unit A&D
Flat Iron Yard
Ayres Street
London SE1 1ES
+44 (0)20 7357 8800
www.urbansalonarchitects.
  com
mail@urbansalonarchitects.
  com
Pages 40ar, 48 both

Vitsoe
shops:
3–5 Duke Street, London
W1U 3ED
+ 44 (0)20 7428 1606
and
33 Bond Street
New York, NY 10012
www.vitsoe.com
Pages 26–27 main, 42

**Wells Mackereth
Architects**
5E Shepherd Street
Mayfair
London W1J 7HP
+44 (0)20 7495 7055
www.wellsmackereth.com
Page 140r

Wickle
24 High Street
Lewes
East Sussex BN7 2LU
+44 (0)1273 487969
www.wickle.co.uk
Page 140l

**Yancey Richardson
Gallery**
535 West 22nd Street
New York, NY 10011
www.yancaeyrichardson.com
Page 68

INDEX

Figures in *italics* indicate captions.

ACKNOWLEDGMENTS

Everyone owns bookshelves, so countless people chipped in with ideas and suggestions, but I am particularly grateful to Nicola Hepworth and Sara Armitage for their recollections of eccentric solutions. In the early stages, Roger Thompson and Colin Davis donated some pithy quotations, and steered me towards useful sources and notable libraries. Jennifer Goulding and Ruth Sleightholme, at *House & Garden* magazine, dug out useful material, in particular pointing me towards Levitate's brilliant stair-cum-bookcase.

I would like to thank all the staff at Ryland Peters & Small who helped the project progress so smoothly: Alison Starling, editorial director, who gave me the opportunity in the first place and helped me thrash out my early ideas; Rebecca Woods, project editor, efficient and accommodating in equal measure; Paul Tilby, designer, for an inspired layout that also fitted in my over-length text; and picture researcher Emily Westlake, for tracking down obscure sources, thereby improving the book immeasurably.

Finally, I give thanks to my family – Michaela, Finlay and Jan – for encouraging me and giving me the time and space to fit all this in around my day job.